Clifford Stoll

HIGH-TECH HERETIC

Clifford Stoll, an MSNBC commentator, lecturer, and a Berkeley astronomer, is the author of the *New York Times* bestseller *The Cuckoo's Egg* and *Silicon Snake Oil: Second Thoughts on the Information Highway.* He lives with his family in the San Francisco Bay Area.

Also by Clifford Stoll

The Cuckoo's Egg

Silicon Snake Oil

High-Tech Heretic

Clifford Stoll

ANCHOR BOOKS

A Division of Random House, Inc. • New York

High-Tech Heretic

Tech

Heretic

Reflections of a Computer Contrarian

FIRST ANCHOR BOOKS EDITION, SEPTEMBER 2000

Copyright © 1999 by Clifford Stoll

All rights reserved under International and Pan-American Copyright Conventions.
Published in the United States by Anchor Books, a division of Random House, Inc.,
New York, and simultaneously in Canada by Random House of Canada Limited,
Toronto. Originally published in hardcover in the United States by Doubleday,
a division of Random House, Inc., New York, in 1999.

Anchor Books and colophon are registered trademarks of Random House, Inc.

The Library of Congress has cataloged the Doubleday edition as follows:

Stoll, Clifford.
High-tech heretic: why computers don't belong in the classroom and
other reflections by a computer contrarian / Clifford Stoll. —1st ed.
p.   cm.
Includes index.
ISBN 0-385-48975-7
1. Computer-assisted instruction.   2. Computers and civilization.
3. Internet (Computer network) in education.   I. Title.
LB1028.5.S77   1999
371.33'4—dc21   99-31141
CIP

Anchor ISBN 0–385–48976–5

Author photograph © Maggie Hallahan
Book design by Charles B. Hames

www.anchorbooks.com

Printed in the United States of America
10   9   8   7   6   5   4   3

To my children

Contents

Introduction

Yes, I'm critical of computing, but I'm not down on technology. Computers don't bother me—hey, I've programmed them since the mid sixties. Like other slaves to the modem, I regularly spend hours facing a monitor.

Rather, the culture that enshrines computers gives me the heebie-jeebies. I worry about a naive credulity in the empty promises of the cult of computing. I'm saddened by a blind faith that technology will deliver a cornucopia of futuristic goodies without extracting payment in kind.

Beyond this, I'm concerned that computers and networks are promoted for their apparent utility, yet we mainly use them for entertainment. Now, there may be nothing wrong with spending an evening on-line, but be honest about it: Don't call three hours of playing Myst useful or educational.

It'd be easy for me to join the crowd crowing about the new electronic frontier. I've been on the Internet since the mid seventies and helped it grow from an obscure R&D project into a worldwide communications phenomenon. And yes, I recognize plenty of neat projects happening on-line. Daily, I hear breathless reporters eager to tell of the latest Web sites. I often meet people who tell me how the Internet solved their problems. Heck, I use it for my astronomy work.

But if you haven't had your fill of wondrous praise for the glorious world of computers and the Internet, just pick up a copy of any computer magazine. Or tune in to any of the computer channels for live coverage from the electronic frontier.

I see my role as injecting—perhaps without success—a few notes of skepticism into the utopian dreams of a digital wonderland. For I believe that techies have a responsibility to challenge hyperbole, false promises, and gross exaggerations.

It's easy to talk about computers' speed, memory, and novelty. More difficult to grapple with the frustrations they generate, their costs (both obvious and indirect), and their side effects. Yet these downsides may be more important than the overhyped benefits. What's lost when we adopt new technologies? Who's marginalized? What valuable things get trampled?

Mind you, I value skepticism, not cynicism. It's easy to be cynical—"I don't believe any of that stuff . . ." On-line, I read plenty of cynical comments directed at government, religion, and community leaders. From cynicism grow disenchantment and apathy.

In turn, I expect skepticism directed at me. I sure don't have Truth in a full nelson, and I'm often perplexed if not completely ambivalent. I'm not trying to convince anyone of my rightness—instead, I yearn for a wider discussion over the claims and promises of computing.

So this isn't an anti-technology manifesto. I own a bunch of computers and regularly log on. I don't intend to heave my CPU out the window or to live in a cave (although I do own a carbide lamp, left over from my spelunking days). My skepticism grows from a love for computing, from a wish to make our technological world better suited for people, rather than people better suited for machines.

Many of my comments deal with computers in education. I shrug when businesses blow fortunes on dubiously useful geegaws, but I'm furious to watch our schools sold down the river of technology. Throngs of educators, lemming-like, line up to wire their schools. Parents grin as they plunk down credit cards to buy electronic machines for their children, anticipating their kids getting a jump start or a quick fix. Meanwhile English teachers must deal with the cry for computer literacy while coping with semiliterate students itching to play with computers who can't read a book.

There's a difference between having access to information and having the savvy it takes to interpret it. Lacking critical thinking, kids are on-screen innocents who confuse form with content, sense with sensibility, ponderous words with weighty thought.

Sure, kids love computers. I met an eighth grader who

happily told me that he'd spent his summer vacation logged on to the Internet for seven hours a day. Every day of the summer. A thirteen-year-old girl looked at me with a straight face and asked, "How can I meet boys if I'm not on-line?"

A computer can't replace a good teacher. But that's what happens when a fifty-minute class gets diluted with a fifteen-minute computer break.

How about computers replacing bad teachers? Again, nope: Bad teachers ought to be replaced with good teachers.

I believe that a good school needs no computers. And a bad school won't be much improved by even the fastest Internet links. That a good teacher can handle her subject without any multimedia support. That the enjoyment of scholarship has nothing to do with making learning fun. That it's unnecessary—and misleading—to push children's work onto the Internet. That students, justifiably, recognize computer assignments primarily as entertainment, rather than education.

The measure of quality of a college has nothing to do with counting computers or ethernet ports. I believe that a student can turn in a good report without clipart, hypertext, or Internet references. That school art should center on creating, not viewing images of museum masterpieces. That a quality library must be centered on books and periodicals. That librarians—not information specialists or database administrators—should be running our libraries. That in times of shrinking education budgets and librarian layoffs, it's an outrage to pour limited funds into fast-obsoleted computers.

Do I sound unreasonable? Fanatic? I don't think so. How

come we so rarely debate whether it's best to spend huge sums of money on computers in schools? Do our students learn more from the Internet or from field trips to forests, museums, and factories? At minimum, we should ask: What problems are solved by bringing the Internet into every school? And what problems might be created when we spend even more time connected to electronic devices?

Schools aside, I'm fascinated by the side effects of computers: How software designed to enhance lectures winds up making lectures even more boring. Why the planned obsolescence of the 1950s has been reincarnated in the world of high tech. That the Internet, rather than bringing us together, works to separate us from those we're closest to.

I'm not afraid of computers. And I don't think our society suffers from the fear of technology. If anything, our problems are rooted in a love affair with gizmos. We've been sold the idea that just around the corner, there's a better invention that'll solve the problems brought on by today's technology.

Skeptical? Yep. But I haven't tossed out my computer. Yet.

1.

Why Computers Don't Belong in the Classroom

A Literate Luddite?

Am I the only one scratching my head over the relentless invocation of the cliché "computer literacy"? Is a supermarket checkout clerk computer literate because he operates a laser scanner, a digital scale, and a networked point-of-sale computer? Is my sister computer literate because she uses a word processor? Are the mirthless robots at the corner arcade computer literate because they reflexively react to Nintendo droids?

Our nation now spends about three billion dollars a year to wire our classrooms, with an aim of making our country's students computer literate. But how much computing does a high school student need to know?

I'd say a high school graduate, intent on going to college, should be able to use a word processor, manipulate a spreadsheet, know what a database does, be able to use e-mail, and know how to browse the World Wide Web.

But not every high school graduate needs to be able to program spreadsheets or lay out databases. It's a waste of time to teach competency on specific programs . . . software taught in high school probably won't be used elsewhere, or will soon be outdated. Instead, we should teach what a database does and where it's useful, so that if that student winds up running a warehouse or keeping an address book, she'll know to turn to a database program.

So, how long did it take you to learn a word processor? A day? Maybe three? Aside from the mechanical typing lessons, this just isn't challenging stuff.

To cover what I've outlined is hardly difficult—perhaps a few weeks on a computer. Unworthy of much time or academic attention. Learning how to use a computer—as opposed to programming a computer—is essentially a mechanical task, one that doesn't require or encourage creativity.

Of course, using a computer requires learning to type. Oops, I mean acquiring keyboarding proficiency. Again, hardly rocket science.

Computer literacy doesn't demand the same level of instruction as English, American history, or physics. It doesn't require the same amount of effort, either. Spending semesters teaching computing simply subtracts time from other subjects.

Probably because computers are so easy for students to learn, educators love to teach computer techniques. But what are their students prepared for? A lifetime of poking at a keyboard for eight hours a day. It's one more way to dumb down the school, giving the appearance of teaching futuristic subjects while dodging truly challenging topics.

Today, practically all office workers know word processing. Most learned it late in life, well past age eighteen. But some subjects, while easy for a child to learn, are impossible for adults . . . languages, for instance. The earlier you start, the easier to become fluent. Same with playing a musical instrument. Or drawing. Or public speaking. Gymnastics. Plenty of people wish they'd learned a musical instrument or a foreign language as a child. But I've never heard anyone complain that they were deprived because they weren't exposed enough to computers or television as a kid.

Which gives you more advantages in business: having a long history of computer experiences, going back to programming Logo? Or fluency in Japanese, German, French, and Chinese? Which is more likely to lead to a rich, happy life: a childhood of Nintendo and Playstations, or one of hikes and bikes?

When I point out the dubious value of computers in schools, I hear the point "Look, computers are everywhere, so we have to bring them into the classroom."

Well, automobiles are everywhere too. They play a damned important part in our society and it's hard to get a job if you can't drive. Cars account for more of our economy than do computers: General Motors' revenues are many times those of Microsoft.

But we don't teach automobile literacy. Nor do we make driver's education a central part of the curriculum—indeed, many schools are now dropping driver's ed, recognizing that teenagers can learn to drive without intensive schooling.

Sure, cars and computers play a prominent role in our lives. Hey—soft-drink ads dominate our skylines and our globe's awash in a syrupy, brown sugar solution, yet we don't push Coca-Cola into elementary schools. At least, we didn't until educators invited Channel-1 and the advertising-laden Internet into classrooms.

But since computers seem ubiquitous, don't we have to bring them to school? Well, no. Television, which is certainly omnipresent, has been relegated to a fairly minor role in education, and politicians aren't funding new initiatives to buy more classroom TV sets.

Want a nation of dolts? Just center the curriculum on technology—teach with videos, computers, and multimedia systems. Aim for highest possible scores on standardized tests. Push aside such less vocationally applicable subjects as music, art, and history. Dolts are what we'll get.

Mathematician Neal Koblitz recognizes the anti-intellectual appeal of computers: "They're used in the classroom in a way that fosters a golly-gee-whiz attitude that sees science as a magical black box, rather than as an area of critical thinking. Instead of asking whether or not technology can support the curriculum, educators try to find ways to squeeze the curriculum into a mold so that computers and calculators can be used."

Computers encourage students to turn in visually exciting hypermedia projects, often at the expense of written compositions and hand-drawn projects. Pasting a fancy graphic into a science report doesn't mean an eighth grader has learned anything. Nor does a downloaded report from the Internet suggest that a student has any understanding of the material.

Yet the emphasis on professional reports sends students the message that appearance and fonts mean more than content. Kids stuck with pencils feel somehow inferior and out of place next to those with computer-generated compositions. The computer-enabled students spend more time preening their reports, rather than understanding the subject matter.

At a high school science fair, I saw a multicolor map of the Earth, showing global temperature distributions. I asked the report's author why the Amazon rain forest seemed so cold—the map showed the jungle to be thirty-eight degrees. "I don't know," he shrugged. "I found the map from the Internet." The guy never considered that the data might be in Celsius, rather than Fahrenheit.

For most high school work—and certainly in elementary grades—searching for on-line source materials not only isn't necessary, it's often antiproductive. I'd rather read a sixth grader's composition on butterflies written after watching a monarch chrysalis in a field of milkweed than view a multimedia display referencing the latest entomological research downloaded from the Internet.

Say that you can have both? Well, the downloaded time-lapse movie clip of a butterfly, complete with enhanced color and synthesized music, certainly makes watching the real thing seem slow-paced and boring. By compressing natural events into unnatural animations, we discourage study, reflection, and observation.

When I teach astronomy to sixth graders, I start with an evening under the stars, not by passing out floppy disks crammed with Hubble Space Telescope images. A love of astronomy—an awe of the universe—begins by looking at the heavens, not by staring into cyberspace.

Who stands to gain from this computer literacy movement? The corporations promoting the wiring of our schools, of course; including almost every telephone company, communications firm, and media outlet. What do these companies know—or care—about childhood development and education?

Professor Douglas Sloan of Teachers College of Columbia University writes, "It doesn't take a flaming Bolshevik, nor even a benighted neo-Luddite, to wonder whether all those computer companies and related textbook publishers that are mounting media campaigns for computer literacy . . . really have the interests of children and young people as their primary concern."

It's impossible to browse the Web without swimming a river of flashing advertisements. Corporations have found the ideal electronic entryway into the classroom: the perfect way to target kids for cereals, candy bars, and clothes.

Yet try to oppose the juggernaut of computer literacy and you're branded a Luddite, lunatic, or reactionary. One librarian who serves on several California technology committees wrote that she feels like the sole voice calling for restraint. "I'm often looked at as crazy when I offer any opposition to computer acquisition."

She notices the disturbing side effects to our emphasis on computing: "Many technologically savvy kids are missing out on vocabulary and the ancillary knowledge necessary to be a well-rounded, educated person."

Other teachers pick this up as well. Patrick Sheehan builds Web sites and teaches a two-hour high school class in multimedia design in Wilsonville, Oregon. Although a computer sharpie, pumped up on both teaching and computing, he writes, "I'm constantly surprised at the level of educational dullness exhibited in student projects. It's frustrating when I want to recommend a student for an internship in the design field, only to find that he can't spell 'school.' This actually happened in one of my student-built multimedia presentations.

"The student's mother talked with me, soon after her son dropped out of school (excuse me . . . skool). Seems that mine was the only class he found interesting enough to attend. I suggested that her son should study English, math, and science, rather than take another multimedia class. She was not amused. Even after I told her about her son's inability to spell basic words, and his predictable discarding of any photocopied articles or instructions I would give him, she insisted that I recommend another multimedia class for him."

It's easy to mistake familiarity with computers for intelligence, but computer literate certainly doesn't equal smart. And computer illiterate sure doesn't mean stupid.

Which do we need more: computer literacy or literacy?

Makes Learning Fun

Technology promises shortcuts to higher grades and painless learning. Today's edutainment software comes shrink-wrapped in computing's magic mantra: "Makes Learning Fun."

You'll hear it from IBM: "The latest Aptivas have a superior selection of top-rated educational software titles like Kid's Room, an Aptiva exclusive that gives your kids a fun place to learn." The fluff goes on about "extreme multimedia delivers full-screen action, blazing graphics and front-row-center-seat sound, resulting in maximum impact in any application."

Public schools agree. Here's a press release pushing software developed by the Texas Agricultural Extension Service, and aimed at 4-H clubs: "It may sound fishy, but Texas 4th graders now have the opportunity to go fishing for facts on the computer, improve their academic skills, learn how they can conserve water and maintain its quality in the state's lakes and streams and have fun at the same time."

The phrase shows up in promotions for college classes, too: The School of Journalism at University of North Carolina at Chapel Hill teaches a core course in Electronic Information Sources. The class motto: Learning Is Fun.

An Oregon high school student who's spent plenty of time on-line wrote: "I mean if I had a choice to learn in a fun matter or a traditial [sic] book manner I would choice the fun way of learning."

Read the promotion for Western Michigan University software to learn about groundwater: It "uses animation, so learning about Calhoun County is more of a video game than a dry lesson or research project . . ."

Learn on your own. Blazing graphics and maximum impact. Go fishing for facts. Learning will be more of a video game than a lesson. Technology makes learning fun. Just one problem.

It's a lie.

Most learning isn't fun. Learning takes work. Discipline. Commitment, from both teacher and student. Responsibility—you have to do your homework. There's no shortcut to a quality education. And the payoff isn't an adrenaline rush, but a deep satisfaction arriving weeks, months, or years later. Equating learning with fun says that if you don't enjoy yourself, you're not learning.

What good are glitzy gadgets to a child who can't pay attention in class, won't read more than a paragraph, and is unable to write analytically? If we want our children to read books, why direct them to computer screens, where it's painful to read more than a few pages? If kids watch too much TV, why bring multimedia video systems into schools?

These teaching machines direct students away from reading, away from writing, away from scholarship. They dull questioning minds with graphical games where quick answers take the place of understanding, and the trivial is promoted as educational. They substitute quick answers and fast action for reflection and critical thinking. Thinking, after all, involves originality, concentration, and intention.

Computing's instant gratification—built into the learning-is-fun mind-set—encourages intellectual passivity, driven mainly by conditioned amusement. Fed a diet of interactive insta-grat, students develop a distaste for persistence, trial and error, attentiveness, or patience.

This obsession with turning the classroom into a funhouse isn't new. Eighty years ago, Austrian educator Rudolf Steiner wrote, "I've often heard that there must be an education which makes learning a game for children; school must become all joy. The children should laugh all the time and learning will be play. This is the best educational principle to ensure that nothing at all is learned."*

Yep, kids love computers. Indeed, it's mainly adults who are uncomfortable around keyboards and monitors. But just what do children learn from computers?

Turning learning into fun denigrates the most important

* "The Younger Generation" in *Thirteen Lectures* by Rudolf Steiner, 1922.

things we can do in life: to learn and to teach. It cheapens both process and product: Dedicated teachers try to entertain, students expect to learn without working, and scholarship becomes a computer game. When in doubt, turn to the electronic mind-crutch.

Is the main problem of today's children that they haven't enough fun? Are kids really deprived of excitement? Are schoolchildren exposed to too few media messages—so that we must bring them the Internet with still more? Must every classroom lesson be sugarcoated by dancing animatrons and singing cartoon characters? Is the job of our schools to provide additional screen time for students who watch three or four hours of television a night?

"All schools need high-speed Internet connections and the appropriate computer hardware to deliver the latest educational applications . . . equal resources should be directed to the creation of dynamic, 3-D virtual learning environments," says Linda Hahner, president of Out of the Blue Design Company, who's excited that "Given enough tools, children will be able to build and program their own space missions."

Children build their own space missions? I'm impressed when a twelve-year-old carves a balsawood glider.

I saw a program for designing Barbie doll clothes . . . it lets kids select styles, colors, and mix outfits. Naturally, it's advertised as a teaching program, though I wonder exactly what it teaches. How to coordinate colors, perhaps, though the kid selects from a most parsimonious palette. You can't mix paints, can't dye cloth, can't stitch things together. At the end of a session, a child has no idea of the tactile difference between calico and corduroy, silk and sailcloth. Can't sew, either.

Along with a small group of parents, I visited a kindergarten class near San Francisco. The other visitors were immediately taken by the display of computer graphic printouts hung on the wall . . . clipart, designed by professionals and printed out by the children. The teacher, busy showing several children how to run the computer, didn't notice one frustrated child working at the crafts table.

While the visitors chatted about the computers, I watched that six-year-old clumsily fold construction paper into the shape of a house. Struggling with round-nosed scissors, he cut a door, drew windows with a crayon, and pasted the paper onto a base. Near the end of our visit, he completed his project—he called it a firehouse—and proudly showed it to the adults in the room. The teacher gave him a "Go away, I'm busy" nod; none of the other visitors so much as glanced at the boy. You could see his face drop.

Well, yes, a six-year-old's crude firehouse hardly compares with a fancy computer printout. But these parents should have recognized the trivial nature of the computer "art."

Remember B. F. Skinner? By feeding corn to pigeons whenever they behaved the way he wanted, Skinner showed that he could get animals to learn behavior. In the 1950s, he applied his pigeon experiments to humans, creating a new way for people to learn: programmed instruction.

Skinner made machines which would pose questions to students. Correct answers would lead to new topics and further questions; wrong answers caused a review and more questions to answer. It was a primitive form of hypertext—each answer led to another encapsulated lesson. Widely promoted in its day, programmed instruction was supposed to revolutionize education.

Skinner's methods fit well with today's computers. Students peck at their keyboards for dollops of sound and animation; administrators get instant reports; parents hear how their kids now enjoy school. This is supposed to make learning fun, not to mention efficient.

Aah, efficiency in education! Get the student to correctly answer questions. Minimize costs and wasted time. Augment teachers with mechanical and electronic aids. Sugarcoat lessons with extreme multimedia and blazing graphics so that students will happily learn on their own, while having fun in the process.

But programmed instruction flopped. The machine forced kids to regurgitate whatever answers the programmer wanted. There was no place for innovation, creativity, whimsy, or improvisation. Flashing lights simply couldn't take the place of a live teacher's encouragement. We resent being treated like pigeons.

In the wake of Skinner's programmed instruction came even nuttier educational fads—teaching machines, sleep learning, and music-induced hypnotic learning. Anything to make education easy and fun. Despite decades of promotion, they all fizzled.

Think Skinner's ideas are dead? Check out the popular children's software program NFL Math. It's designed around professional football and is supposed to teach arithmetic. "Packed with photo-realistic animations," this program "makes hitting a wide receiver with a pass more fun than hitting the books." It promises such "learning skills" as addition, fractions, statistics, and percentages. The kids get to watch short, poorly animated football segments, interrupted by half-baked math questions ("Which is more yards rushed—1,182 or 1,207?"). Result? Your children will "score better grades in math!" Uh, right.

The program forces the child to do a math problem in order to be rewarded with two minutes of entertainment. Then the torture begins anew. What a great way to teach hatred of math.

NFL Math and its many brethren typically present questions in the format $4+3 = $? They can accept only the obvious answers. Like Skinner's pigeons, you get rewarded for pressing the right button.

A real teacher might well ask, "Seven equals what?" A fascinating question with an infinite number of answers: "Three plus four," "Ten minus three," "Days in a week," "The dwarfs in *Snow White,*" "Number of deadly sins," "The Seven Immortals of the Wine Cup," "The Group of Seven revolutionized Canadian painting," "The number of samurai in Kurosawa's best movie," "The German expression *Siebensachen,* which means the baggage you carry on a trip." These answers, incomprehensible to any computer, make perfect sense to a real teacher . . .

and open up whole fields for creative discussion. What began as an arithmetic question blossoms into a lesson on language, art, science, history, or culture.

New teachers, fresh out of college, seem to be most affected with the connection between gizmos, classrooms, and fun in learning. Ms. Jennifer Donovan, a student teacher from Stetson University, wrote to me, repeating the standard party line: Lessons must be fun in order to compete with television and to motivate students. "In the 1950s, the job market did not call for computer education. But in a changing world, students are hard pressed to find well-paying jobs that do not involve computer technology."

These fit together: Jobs go to those who know computers. Computers motivate students. Students won't learn unless it's fun.

Well, many subjects aren't fun.* I wonder how the fun-to-learn teacher handles the Holocaust, Rape of Nanking, or American slavery. Perhaps her class creates Web sites about these subjects—and the students concentrate on graphic design instead of history. But scholarship isn't about browsing the Internet—it's about understanding events, appreciating history, and interpreting our world.

"But you don't understand," say my techie friends. "Computers are wonderful motivators for students. In this age of television, they won't write or do their homework without one."

---

* Plenty of jobs aren't fun, either.

And so we happily provide computers to students and expect them to suddenly become interested in academic topics. We encourage them to play with the machine . . . any scholastic connection is secondary.

Kids do seem to be motivated by computers. But doesn't that multimedia machine mainly motivate kids to play with the computer, in the same way that television motivates kids to watch more videos?

Motivation—the will to move—comes from yourself. You choose what puts you in motion and causes you to move. Computers cause you to sit in one place and not to move.

Don Tapscott, author of *Growing Up Digital,* sees a new kind of young intellectual explorer who will process information and learn differently than those who came before them. "New media tools offer great promise for a new model of learning—one based on discovery and participation," he says. Thanks to cheap computers, we'll see a shift from teaching to "the creation of learning partnerships and learning cultures. The schools can become a place to learn rather than a place to teach."

The field of educational technology is filled with such empty clichés. In this dreamworld, empowered students eagerly learn from one another, encouraged by teachers who act more like coaches than instructors. We'll replace the sage on the stage with a guide on the side. Exciting on-line expeditions will replace outmoded chalk-and-talk lectures. Student-centered learning will be tutor-led and context-based rather than rote plug-and-chug. Child-centered classrooms. Blah, blah, blah.

Can't blame students for getting sick of teachers lecturing about how the square of the hypotenuse has something to do with the sum of the squares of the legs of a right triangle. We yearn for depth, narrative, passion, involvement. For experience. Along comes the magic machine promising interactive fun. What kid can resist?

And I can't blame teachers for getting sick of students sitting there with mouths agape, not listening but not quite sleeping. Perhaps that's why adults figure that making finger motions on a keyboard is an appropriate activity . . . that something must be happening in the kids' brains. In that sense, computers are parent-pleasing devices: machines to give the appearance of learning and the illusion of interactive, instant information.

Seems clear that an inspiring teacher doesn't need computers; a mediocre teacher isn't improved by one. I've never met a teacher who feels there's too much classroom time— they always complain that the periods are too short and there's too much material to cover.

Teaching, alas, is a low-paid calling. Some teachers attend college and put up with frustrations for a steady pay and eventual retirement. But I'll bet the best teachers are in it for the feedback: the smile on the kid's face and the "Aha" from the chemistry student. These, of course, are the very things that technology removes. The Internet gets the credit and the teacher gets the blame. And that great promised land of low-cost education—distance learning—essentially eliminates interpersonal interaction. Maybe that's why experienced teachers approach computers with hesitation.

In *Teachers and Machines,* Larry Cuban points out that teachers are frequently criticized as Luddites resistant to progress. A century of reformers have blamed the slow introduction of teaching devices on reactionary teaching staff. For instance, Charles Hoban, who worked to introduce instructional radio and TV, said, "The current and historical role of the classroom teacher is highly ritualized." Any change in that ritual is "likely to be resisted as an invasion of the sanctuary by the barbarians . . . Any systematic attempt to scientize and rationalize the intuitively determined interaction patterns of the teacher is likely to elicit at least some teacher hostility and resistance."

That hostility is well justified. Teachers need only open a closet door to find stacks of obsolete and unused teaching gizmos: filmstrips, instructional television systems, Apple II computers, and any number of educational videotapes. Each promised a revolution in the classroom. None delivered.

"Oh, but computers are different from old technologies like radio and television" runs the argument. "Computers are interactive. They're fun!"

Well, just why is electronic interactivity good for scholarship? With a computer, you're interacting with something, not someone. Doubtless, even the worst teacher is more versatile and adaptable than the finest computer program. Come to think of it, aren't teachers interactive? It's hard to think of a classroom without interaction.

The old saw still rings true: What requires the least effort is least cherished. Yet somehow we expect a simple, easy, fun digital education to be both lasting and valuable.

"But the Internet is important to schools," consultants in computer-aided instruction tell me. "It links students straight to famous scientists. They can chat with researchers at observatories and laboratories. And there's instant homework help available on-line."

Well, no. Famous scientists—and obscure ones, too—don't have time to answer e-mail from distant students. Those academics are taking care of their projects, managing post-docs, teaching classes, and writing grant proposals. Astronomers who enjoy working with kids would far prefer to meet the kids, not answer a slew of messages over the net. That inquiring mind directed to the net will likely dead-end in some press release or a mountain of indecipherable jargon.

Teachers have the difficult job of not just understanding a body of academic facts—they must understand their students. The teaching method that connects for one child won't work with another. The student who's strong in one area will certainly be weak in another. What seems like a game to someone will feel like work to another. The intention should be enlightenment, not entertainment.

Learning isn't about acquiring information, maximizing efficiency, or enjoyment. Learning is about developing human capacity. To turn learning into fun is to denigrate the two most important things we can do as humans: To teach. To learn.

The Hidden Price
of Computers

What's the cost of computers in the classroom? Around the country, communities float thirty-year bond issues to buy computers which will be obsolete within five years. Wiring a school typically costs thousands of dollars per classroom; and it will have to be redone within a decade, as communications systems evolve. Classroom software has a surprisingly short life, as curriculum, computers, and educational climate change. Then there's the need for technical support—it's silly to expect English teachers to install and maintain the high school's file servers.

No question that computing is much cheaper than twenty years ago. Yet our schools don't magically get expanded budgets, although it seems as if technology grant money comes free for the asking.

No, there's a finite number of bucks available for education; pushing some into computing means less money for other programs. By insisting that we spend time and money on technological teaching tools, we implicitly reduce the amount of time and money spent on other programs.

Listen to Kathy Popp, technology coordinator for a small, rural community in south central Pennsylvania.

First, Ms. Popp recites the usual clichés: "Chestnut Ridge School District shares a vision with the surrounding community . . . that technology can be the catalyst and agent in changing the way teachers teach and the way students learn. Our vision sees technology as the great equalizer, in a playing field where unequal amounts of money are spent on educating children."

As the Amish leave that area, technology will become both cornucopia and equalizer. How'll they reach this utopia?

"Access and use of the Information Highway is part of this technology. But in order to purchase technology," Ms. Popp writes, "both teachers and district supplies have to be cut."

What? Given a choice between buying computers and hiring teachers, she picks the machines. Indeed, the Internet is so valuable to this rural district that "Workshops have even been held for the secretaries, aides, cooks, and janitors."

Cooks and janitors need Internet training? Do they expect cybercooking and electrocleaning? Ms. Popp continues: "The commitment of our school and community was evident when money was budgeted this school year for a 56 Kilobaud line. A high school teacher position was left unfilled, and supplies were cut. That's commitment to connectivity."

For the price of one less English teacher, her school district now boasts a medium-speed Internet link. In southern Pennsylvania, at least, browsing the Web takes precedence over learning how to write.

Which is more important: Internet or books? Computers or teachers? On-line access or a local clinic? Kathy Popp has no doubt: "We see access to unlimited use on the Information Highway as the books we don't have on our high school library shelves and the experts we don't have in a rural setting. We see it as a health resource in an area which is classified as medically underserved."

Faced with pressing educational and social problems, technology promoters first turn to the Internet. They're blind to other possible solutions, such as more teacher support, better teaching conditions, tighter discipline, more appropriate curricula, or recasting school goals. This obsession with computing tilts community activity as well. There's no reason to improve the library, start a health clinic, or open a community college. Just bring in the Internet.

Perhaps Ms. Popp feels that a half-baked electronic educational casserole is better than nothing. Without the Internet, her students might not be exposed to information which is simply unavailable in rural Pennsylvania.

Well sure, there's plenty on-line that can't be found in the Chestnut Ridge School District. But instead of exploiting what's available locally—the people, color, and history of the region—computer promoters press students to reach into the non-world of cyberspace. Seek answers from the net, not from a teacher or mentor. Build relationships via e-mail, not by meeting people. Explore the Web, not your own community.

What if your school can afford only one computer for a class of twenty-five students? No problem, says Peggy Ratsch, information technology specialist in Baltimore County Public Schools. According to *Education Technology News,* she says that if teachers can show they're using one machine well in the classroom, they are more likely to get funding for more. In other words, get the first computer so that you can get others. Presumably, the aim is every student behind a computer . . . but I doubt that will end Ms. Ratsch's money hunt. Technologists see technology as a solution, never as a problem.

President Clinton announced that a computer in every classroom is a goal of education. Not a means, but a goal. What's wrong with this picture?

If technology is adopted as education's crown jewels, our classrooms naturally change their value structures. At Poly High School in Long Beach, California, the roof leaked big time, and rainwater dripped into the classrooms. What to do? Why, save the computers! The principal sent out a message that teachers could get plastic bags from the main office.

No thought that books, desks, or student projects might be worth saving. Certainly no suggestion that money might be better spent on a new roof which would last thirty years, rather than computers with maybe a five-year life span.

MIT sociology professor Sherry Turkel also favors bringing computers into schools, though she recognizes the limitations. If you just drop a lot of computers into the classroom, "Nothing miraculous is going to happen." And for some areas, the computer isn't the best tool for teaching. "You need a teacher and a conversation to teach the beauty of poetry," she said.

What about science? Well, Professor Turkel's seven-year-old daughter was curious about magnets. The girl had a computer program about magnets but didn't really understand them. Then Professor Turkel bought a magnet for her daughter. "Once she was holding it in her hands, she got it," she said.

Wait a second. This child's in second grade, fluent in computing, yet hasn't played with magnets. What household provides a computer for a kid but not refrigerator magnets?

Same thing happens in schools. Classrooms get plenty of computers and software, but not such things as paper, crayons, blocks, and, yes, magnets. An ISDN line instead of an English teacher.

Here's an anonymous Canadian schoolteacher, quoted by K. Reil at the University of Victoria: "They can give us the ax, but they can spend thousands on computers. We have to fire our music coordinator, we have to fire our music teachers, and we have shitty libraries."

Next time a principal or school board member shows off a modern computer lab in eighth grade, ask this question: "What was in this room before these computers?" Here are the answers I got:

"We converted the library into the computer lab. With the

multimedia encyclopedias, we no longer need as many books."

"Oh, we used to teach art in this room. But we don't anymore."

"This technology lab used to be our carpentry shop."

"A music studio . . ."

And if you think computers only cut into school libraries and music programs, you should check out high school chemistry labs. The days of test tubes and Bunsen burners are fast disappearing, as school districts get scared of students handling chemicals. Too easy to spill acid, burn a finger, or build a bomb. With safety concerns driving up the cost of real chem labs, schools naturally turn to the high-tech solutions: computer simulations.

School chemistry software comes complete with pretty images of thermometers, pipets, and condensers. To simulate a titration, you type in commands, use a mouse to drag a simulated beaker across the screen, and then watch the effect on a simulated pH meter. Sure looks spiffy, but it ain't chemistry. It's simulated chemistry.

Visit the Science Magnet School in Buffalo, New York. Over near Humboldt Park, you'll find dozens of computers, complete with modems and high-resolution monitors. They sponsor their own public access Internet Freenet. But where's the science?

"I volunteered to teach physics there," reports Professor Reichert of the State University of New York at Buffalo. "But this science magnet school has no physics lab. No air table to teach mechanics, no hands-on experiments. All they have is computers."

Across the continent, technology in the classroom equates to computers in the classroom. But plenty of other technological devices are essential for teaching, especially in the sciences. "It fries me that we can get cash for computers but we can't buy an optics workbench, a set of voltmeters, or a collection of tuning forks," steams Dr. Reichert. "At a physics teachers meeting, I met a guy who wouldn't pay two thousand dollars for hands-on apparatus to teach magnetic fields and angular momentum. The same guy happily spent twenty times that much on a roomful of computers."

For the cost of two dozen computers, you can equip a terrific high school physics lab. Ten years from now, when those computers are in the trash heap, a set of tuning forks could still teach resonance, a voltmeter could still demonstrate Ohm's law, and students might still learn about angular momentum using that apparatus.

Biology gets snookered by computers, too. Hey—it's much easier to show computer simulations of growing plants, dissected frogs, and crowded ecosystems. Less messy. No offending animal rights activists either. But the effect of replacing biology lab with computational biology is to eviscerate the science and eliminate the sense of exploration and discovery that leads to understanding.

But don't real physicists, chemists, and biologists use computers? Sure. But they didn't learn their professional skills on software. Nor did their schools teach science using simulations.

Computer simulations are powerful tools used across the sciences. They yield answers to specific questions. But they don't give understanding, can't demonstrate what it means to do science, won't inspire the curiosity essential to becoming a scientist. They teach simulated science.

There's a bizarre system of grant evaluation that encourages—if not demands—that all new applications have something to do with technology in the classroom. Inevitably, educators apply for computer grants to get money to use elsewhere, say to hire assistants or buy supplies. A screwy way to fund our schools.

Other educators use this money-for-technology fountain as a Trojan mouse. Tell the public that we're bringing computers into the schools; meanwhile sneak in problem-based learning, collaborative learning, or constructivist education. Reformers see technology as a back door through which they'll shake up traditional classrooms. At best, it's an expensive—if disingenuous—way to reform our schools. At worst, it's outright fraud: selling a hidden agenda on the promise that technology will improve our schools.

There's one area of education where computers have been widely accepted: It's a rare school administrator without a desktop computer. Principals find 'em ideal for tracking attendance, following student grades, making calendars, and writing form letters to parents. As in larger society, educational computing works great at automating administration.

So shouldn't computers reduce school costs by making administrative activities more efficient? I wish it were so. As computers become widely adopted in elementary and high schools, they add a whole new layer of school administrators and middle managers. These include technicians to keep the machines running, content administrators to watch over what the students see, and technology specialists to teach teachers how to best use the digital machines. Save money? Naw.

As schools become networked, I expect teachers' classbooks and attendance rolls to become centralized databases. This won't make the job of teaching any easier, of course. Rather, administrators will gather more information about students (and teachers), generate more paperwork, and further constrain creative teachers. Who'll be happiest? Principals who work in their offices, rather than visiting with teachers, students, and parents. Students who enjoy working alone. Teachers who are more comfortable behind a keyboard than in front of a chalkboard.

But then, teachers may be a disappearing breed. Just as librarians call themselves "information specialists," school systems increasingly hire "information technology professionals" and "technology coordinators." These people search out new ways to use these gizmos, while simultaneously hustling grants for more technostuff.

No surprise, then, to hear that any classroom without a computer is somehow inferior. Peter Hutcher, technology director of the Oakland, California, school district, says, "We have an obligation to provide access to the Internet for students. If they don't have it at home, we darn well better provide it during the school day." Here's Ms. Popp again: "Every day that our children do not have access to the Information Highway is one day less of an excellent education for them."

What nonsense. You certainly can get an excellent education without a computer. And schools don't have a duty to provide Internet access. They have a duty to provide an education.

Is access to television—even children's educational television—necessary to obtain an excellent education? Do schools have an obligation to provide TV to those who don't have it at home?

As much as I love computers, I can't imagine getting an excellent education from any multimedia system. Rather than augmenting the teacher, these machines steal limited class time and direct attention away from scholarship and toward pretty graphics.

Really want to improve classroom teaching? Give teachers more preparation time. Prep time used to be for grading homework and setting up classwork; today, it's increasingly eaten by computers. Each program—even the simplest—requires someone to get the computers ready . . . inevitably, it's the teacher. For the dirty secret of educational technology is that computers waste teachers' time, both in and out of the classroom.

No amount of Web searching can make up for a lack of critical thinking or communications skills. No multimedia computer will help a student develop analytic abilities. No microprocessor can augment the creative interplay of hand, clay, and art teacher. No on-line astronomy program can engender the same sense of awe as first seeing the rings of Saturn through a telescope. No computer will encourage a budding athlete to run faster, kick harder, or jump higher.

With or without a computer, a mediocre instructor will never kindle a love for learning. And a good teacher doesn't need the Internet to inspire her students to excellence.

Loony for Laptops

For most of the twentieth century, technology promoters have sought to eliminate textbooks.

Here's Thomas Alva Edison in 1922: "The motion picture is destined to revolutionize our educational system . . . in a few years it will supplant largely, if not entirely, the use of textbooks."

A decade later, Benjamin Darrow, founder of the Ohio School of the Air, wrote: "The central and dominant aim of education by radio is to bring the world to the classroom, to make universally available the services of the finest teachers, the inspiration of the greatest leaders . . . unfolding world events through the radio may come as a vibrant and challenging textbook of the air."

In 1945, William Levenson wrote in *Teaching Through Radio:* "A portable radio receiver will be as common in the classroom as is the blackboard. Radio instruction will be integrated into school life as an accepted educational medium."

California State University Chancellor Barry Munitz, in 1995, proposed to build a new campus with no library. "Why bother wasting all that money on bricks and mortar when it could be better spent on technology for getting information via computer?"

And in 1998, then Speaker of the House Newt Gingrich spoke to the Supercomm trade show: "We'll replace textbooks with computers. I hope within five years they will have no more textbooks."

These techno-promoters speak with technologically forked tongues: They'll advance literacy by eliminating books. They'll have us believe that movies, radio, television, and computers will somehow teach our children to love reading without ever having to touch a page. Our educational revolutionaries pay lip service to the need to read, but wish to channel students into a substitute for reading.

Why this deep distrust of books?

According to the chairman of the Texas State Board of Education, Jack Christie, replacing textbooks with computers will solve important school problems. For him, outdated and boring books are the enemy of a quality education. In 1996 he said, "We were replacing social studies textbooks that had the Berlin Wall still up, Russia as one country, and Ronald Reagan finishing his second term."

Never mind that only an idiot would teach current events

from a textbook. Today, classroom computers have become a political panacea for school problems.

Loopy as it sounds, plenty of school districts are seriously considering tossing out textbooks and buying laptop computers for their students. The school board of Earlimart, California, spent $3,000,000 on portable computers, then went $836,000 over its yearly budget for software, scanners, and modems. In Kent, Connecticut, the school district bought a laptop computer for every seventh grader. Same with the sixth graders in New York's Washington Heights Public School IS 218.

How come? Many of these programs come titled with educator-speak: "Anytime-Anywhere Learning," "Cutting-Edge Classrooms," "Internet Empowerment," "Extending Technology Infrastructure."

Below the buzzwords, promoters give five reasons for replacing textbooks with portable computers. Portable computers will be mobile, letting kids learn anywhere. Those laptops can be updated instantly . . . no more out-of-date textbooks. The laptop computers will outlast books because they'll always have new information. School boards will save money by avoiding buying new books. Interactive software will engage television-bound students. There's a grain of truth in each of these claims. And a hunk of falsehood.

Laptop computers are promoted as a great way for kids to learn anyplace. After all, they're portable. Well, which is more mobile, a laptop computer or a book? Which can you use on the bus, subway, or park bench? Which can you leave unattended at the stadium seat or the Laundromat? Which needs neither batteries nor cables? Which is really available anytime and anywhere: the book or the computer?

Nor are student-assigned computers particularly mobile when, as we'll see, they must be accompanied by parents to and from school.

Laptop computers can be instantly updated? Well, sure: just download the latest software or connect to the right Web page. Pop in the CD-ROM that came in the mail.

But frequent updating of classroom materials simply isn't necessary. Core academic content changes slowly. Indeed, the past two decades of research haven't greatly changed basic high school math, physics, and chemistry. If you learned these fields up to the late 1970s, you're perfectly able to understand today's trends and changes. Once we exclude politically inspired curriculum changes, I'll bet the same's true for the great bulk of English, social studies, geography, and biology.

Do we need textbooks to be instantly updated? Should schoolchildren be held responsible for the latest events and current research? Is it important that a ninth grader's science project reference reports from the past few months?

I'd be impressed if a science fair project shows an understanding of simple harmonic motion, a concept that's two hundred years old. More often, alas, high school science projects merely echo recent research in science. Even worse, more and more science projects simply show computer animations of someone else's experiment. We tell students that their projects must be up-to-the-minute, complete with animated graphics, but we don't teach them fundamental science. We'll show them animated test tubes, yet won't ask them to actually mix (and taste) vinegar and baking soda.

Moreover, for every obsolete book, there's a Web site that's inaccurate, out of date, one-sided, or no longer maintained. For all that educators grinch about textbooks (and there's plenty to complain about!) at least someone's reviewed them for content, applicability, grade level, accuracy, and balance. That's simply not true of 99 percent of what's on the Web. Giving students the latest information has little to do with presenting them with quality information or well-organized lessons.

Portable computers have far shorter lives than textbooks. In the hands of most kids, I'll bet most laptops won't last three semesters. They can't survive a drop onto a concrete sidewalk, a visit to a sandy beach, a splash of muddy slush, or a squashed backpack. They don't like being left in hot cars and freezing blizzards. Their CD-ROMs can't handle peanut butter and jelly. Their rechargeable batteries need annual replacement. And if the kids don't break 'em, they're obsolete within five years.

Now contrast a ten-year-old textbook with a ten-year-old computer. The history book still covers a massive amount of human history but misses a decade of current affairs. The ten-year-old computer simply doesn't work—you can't get any software for it. It's landfill.

A well-written textbook will last a decade; the poorly written one shouldn't get past the school board. Not true for Web pages and computer programs: Even the best software demands frequent updates. And cruddy programs and lousy Web sites glide right past administrators.

Could schools save money by replacing textbooks with computers? The economics work out something like this: Texas, with 3.8 million public school students, spends $1.8 billion to buy textbooks for the next six years. That's about $80 per student per year. Add that up for six or seven years and it's enough to buy a laptop computer for every student.

It's an administrator's dream. Don't pour money down the drain on textbooks—spend it on portable computers, assign one to every student, and periodically upload new material to each machine. Jack Christie estimates that each computer can be updated for a dollar or so.

Yet so far, schools that have adopted computers find that they cost way more than textbooks. In Kent, Connecticut, the computer budget is over four times that allocated for textbooks. How come?

To begin with, a laptop computer won't last six years. Heck, school lunch boxes don't last six years. School districts wind up replacing portable computers faster than they're now replacing textbooks.

Then, too, laptop computers have complex demands, which translate into expensive operation. First, routine maintenance: keyboards wear out, chargers and cables get lost, software needs to be installed. Then the all too familiar non-routine problems: disk crashes, broken displays, and spilt Cokes gumming up the CD-ROM drive. Hey—replacement batteries alone will run over twenty dollars per year.

The technical needs of the computer create a new bureaucratic bumpf of technicians, computer coordinators, and information specialists. These people tend not to teach, but to fix machines, buff the school's high-tech image, and promote high-tech pedagogy.

Unlike books, computers have street value. Plenty of kids have been mugged for their lunch money. Schoolyard bullies and neighborhood punks sure won't ignore the second grader with a portable computer. Assigning valuable objects to schoolchildren makes the kids walking targets. Makes classrooms attractive to thieves.

Kids misplace books. Swimsuits. Glasses. They leave trumpets on the school bus. Give them laptop computers and they'll lose them as well. It's absurd to expect every school kid to be responsible.

Once you buy a book, you needn't spend a nickel maintaining it. For a computer, the initial cost is the cheap part. Schools will have to tack on constant maintenance: batteries, software, upgrades, and repairs. When a teenager drops a book, it still works. When a ten-year-old steps on a history text, it doesn't need a new hundred-dollar display module. Who would break into a high school locker to steal an English textbook?

Schools will waste money on software, too. Someone has to write new programs and create Web sites that meet the requirements of the board of education. Software publishers sure won't do it for free. Today, a typical educational software title costs somewhere between twenty-five and seventy-five dollars . . . about the same as a textbook. Will the state school board hire a group of computer programmers to write programs which fully cover the curriculum? Hard to imagine that this'll save money, when it costs some half million dollars to make one CD-ROM title.

School boards would love to rely on the ocean of public domain software. But teachers who have tried to use freeware complain about incorrect information, misspelled words, and inappropriate pedagogy. Nobody's responsible for keeping the programs updated as curriculum demands change. And without professional organization, they're hard to fit into statewide requirements. Unless the school board pays someone to write, organize, review, and cull software, the schools have to rely on the spotty efforts of hobbyists and non-professionals.

Educators like to say that the computer won't replace textbooks—it will augment or supplement them. If that's so, then the economic argument is all backward: You'll wind up buying computers, software, and books.

Jack Christie sees computers as the way to keep Texas students from becoming information haves and information have-nots. "The poor child has an equal knowledge base as the child in the lah-de-dah high school." Odd, isn't it, that both suburban and urban schools use identical textbooks. Books aren't the cause of whatever inequalities he's referring to.

And if there's one thing that will discourage poor students, it's a monthly charge imposed on their parents for a laptop computer. In Beaufort, South Carolina, for example, donations from businesses help subsidize students to lease laptops for fifteen dollars a month. But not all students can afford that, so a new rich-poor gap is created where there didn't used to be one—the well-off kids tote laptops, the poor ones don't.

One effect of the intense pressure to bring technology into schools is that computers have become status symbols for children. Karen Marshall used to work as a computer classroom aide in New Jersey. Some of her students were embarrassed to say they didn't own a computer or hadn't the skills that other children had. "I had some kids who had never touched a computer but didn't want to admit it," she said. "There's a lot of pressure to be computer literate and the majority of kids don't want to admit it if they can't do it."

When Dr. Christie presented his plan to equip students with laptops to the Texas State Legislature, some forty speakers supported him. Some were educators, many were computer salesmen. About the only one speaking against the idea was Gary Chapman of the University of Texas at Austin.

"There was a fair amount of pure Texas hucksterism on display," Mr. Chapman reports. "One vendor poured water on a laptop to show its durability, then invited a portly legislator to jump on the machine. Another demonstrated a software product that, inexplicably, turned ordinary addition problems into animated cartoons."

Picking up on those cartoons, Dr. Christie, a chiropractor, said, "This is the Nintendo generation. Students get bored when they read about geometry from a textbook, but become motivated when they see three-dimensional software with 'living triangles.'"

Living triangles will motivate students? I'll bet most will recognize those dancing geometric figures as superficial edutainment, a cheap substitute for a quality geometry lesson.

Those three-dimensional graphics will motivate about the same way that a television show motivates. By showing, rather than doing.

Nope, the textbook won't be as much fun as playing Nintendo, nor be as animated as the CD-ROM game. Books require exercising imagination and down-home work. Working out mathematics problems with a pencil doesn't compare with a glitzy arcade with colorful patterns. Dr. Christie's "living triangles" turn geometry into a game.

Do we look forward to the day when chiropractors, nurses, and physicians learn their trade from animated cartoons, replete with living triangles? Who can best inspire a love for history: Mickey Mouse or a competent social studies teacher? Which is more important, learning how Microsoft formats words or how Shakespeare formats words?

Remember that it's painful to read a book on a computer screen. Hypertext, the non-linear computerized substitute for the printed word, defeats any attempt at a narrative. How can you tell a story when the reader treats a work as a computer game?

Indeed, while hypertext and computer games can have any number of endings, a story can have but a single ending. And our most important stories—our lives—run linearly, from birth to death, with each hour following the previous one. The narrative of my life doesn't jump from one alternative reality to another.

No doubt that it's more fun to play with amusing CD-ROMs and surf the Web than to actually work through trigonometry problems or read Shakespeare. But a love of books—a yearning to read—can't grow from staring at computer screens. Rather, we can look forward to a generation of functional illiterates, for whom books are little more than ink on wood pulp.

If you want to engage students in learning how to survey an oil field, you're better off tossing out both textbook and laptop. Invest in a live-wire teacher; one that knows triangles, trigonometry, and transits. One that'll tromp across the grassland with a bunch of high school kids in tow. If you want a student to understand geometry, don't buy her expensive 3-D software. Instead, give her paper, ruler, compass, and a teacher who'll get her to check up on Pythagoreas. That's motivation. Entertainment, of a sort, too.

Giving a laptop computer to every Texas schoolchild will certainly teach computer literacy. Okay, what skills do you need to run an educational computer program? Not much: the ability to type and move a mouse. It's about the same as watching television with a remote control . . . you point and click. Passively, you absorb (or ignore) what's presented on the screen.

The very skills taught by television are reinforced by educational software. Sit, watch, and be entertained. More than anything else, computers teach children that the world is a preprogrammed place, a virtual universe where solving a problem means clicking on the right icon.

A lack of computer literacy simply isn't a major problem among those now attending school. Dr. Christie's Nintendo generation is certainly well equipped to handle computers in the coming years. Doubtless, they're more computer literate than any other generation.

As computers replace textbooks, students will become more computer literate and more book illiterate. They'll be exploring virtual worlds, watching dancing triangles, downloading the latest Web sites. But they won't be reading books.

Just how well do computers fit into a classroom? Michael Stoll (sadly, not a relation to this author) watched a laptop-equipped sixth grade in New York City. Writing in *The Christian Science Monitor,* he reports on New York Public School IS 218. In partnership with software and computer makers, their school board provided laptop computers to Washington Heights sixth graders.

Mr. Stoll reports no worries about children having their portable computers robbed. Each family is required to pay ten dollars per month for an insurance policy covering the kid's computer. That policy stipulates that laptops may leave school only when accompanied by an adult. If the family falls behind in payments, the computer doesn't go home.

Since the computers can't leave school without an adult, squads of parents escort the sixth graders home. Parents have organized escort patrols to accompany the kids to and from school. "We know where they are every minute of every day," says Giulia Cox, laptop-program coordinator. "We joke that these are the most cared-for kids in the New York school system."

If the main effect of the laptop computer program is to

increase parental involvement, maybe it's worth the money. But how long the parents will continue to act as chaperones is anyone's guess. I wonder how the kids feel—sixth graders of my generation would be mortified if their folks had to walk 'em home.

The real problems show up when you watch a lesson being taught. It seems like normal classroom learning, except everything takes way longer.

The teacher doesn't call out, "Everyone take out your pencil and paper." Instead, it's "Everyone open up your Targus case and put your laptops on your desk. Now plug in your machine and boot it." You wait as two dozen machines come to life. "Now launch Microsoft Word." A minute later, most of the students look up. "Okay, now open up the file that you worked on last week."

What ought to take thirty seconds now swallows five minutes, if everything goes well. One morning, a student couldn't get Windows to run because his computer had picked up a virus. That distraction cost the class another ten minutes, as the teacher struggled to get the machine to work.

The most trivial bugs waste everyone's time. But ordinary lessons soon dissolve into computer training. The science class about pendulums involved swinging a weight on a string. The actual experiment took three minutes. But the teacher needed almost a quarter hour to explain how to make a chart in Microsoft Word.

"I don't think they're slowing down my classroom so much

anymore because I don't use them," says Kevin Kinkade, the science teacher. His students now complete their computer assignments at home.

These aren't incompetent, computer illiterate teachers. One was hired for his background and enthusiasm for the little gray boxes. All have taken a ten-hour training seminar in Microsoft software. Yet few of these teachers are sold on the idea.

"If you can't read, write, and do math, what good is a computer?" asks Sarah Pitari, the sixth-grade math teacher. "The laptop is a novelty. The essence of the program is being lost."

"I get more work out of them in pen and paper," says Valerie Valentine, who teaches humanities. "It's not helping them to learn how to read. I'm not sure exactly what it's helping them to learn, if anything."

Theresa Velazquez also teaches humanities and sees a real advantage to the laptop program. "The children are very excited," she says. "You can see the brightness in their faces. Children have a way with computers."

Tapping their laptop computers, kids can't draw diagrams with a pencil. Instead, they use a computer drawing program—which wastes time and distracts them from the concept at hand.

Not that they need to take notes—plenty of handouts are available over the network. Alternatively, kids can copy someone else's artwork over the computer. Result—the sixth graders don't take many notes . . . a crude sketch shows understanding; someone else's artwork shows someone else's ideas.

Maybe these students don't need hand drawings or marginal comments. Perhaps they constantly refer to their word-processed handouts. Maybe they can take notes on a keyboard without disturbing those nearby. Maybe they can sit through a less-than-stellar lecture without fooling with that fancy desktop toy. Possibly these kids don't run computer games when the class gets boring. I'll bet otherwise.

Indeed—teachers commonly catch students surreptitiously playing video games during class. "I play Mortal Kombat, Trilogy, and Rat Man," said one sixth grader. "I want Resident Evil, but I can't afford it."

In past years, kids didn't hand in their homework. Now, according to proud administrators, they're motivated. The star student spends two hours every night playing a business-management game on her computer.

"It's fun because it's a better way to learn," she says. "Some kids think it's boring to read. With laptops they're going to be much more into homework."

No doubt: Compared to running games on a computer, reading is boring. If homework means playing computer games, kids will love it. Who'd read a book when Mortal Kombat is just a keystroke away?

"I've just about stopped using the computer in class, because the kids are so distracted by the computers themselves," Ms. Valentine concludes. "I think it's the corporate world manipulating the public school system. It's a big show."

The obsession of educators with laptop computers extends beyond elementary and high school. The University of North

Carolina recently decided that they will provide each undergrad with a particular Intel laptop computer from a specific computer maker. The program, of course, isn't advertised as a tuition increase, but rather as a boon for the students. The undergrads know better.

"Nobody in charge has even begun to address how they expect these computers to help educate students," writes Drew Gilmore, an undergrad. "The whole thing looks like an attempt to bring up the school's national rankings." He worries about the disruptions caused by three hundred laptops in a lecture hall, as well as increased crime on campus. Anyway, who says that a journalism major needs the same computer as a physics or engineering student? What about those undergrads who already own laptop computers made by Apple, for whom the required software is incompatible?

Even in graduate education, administrators want to foist standardized computers onto students. Robert May, Dean of the University of Texas Business School, expects wonderful effects from requiring all graduate students to buy a 233 MHz Dell laptop computer. He spouts the usual babble about "tremendous cultural effects" and "productivity and learning effects." Then he tells of students "exploiting their community in terms of collaboration, knowledge sharing, and file sharing." It will "bind the class together as a learning community . . . It will be one more factor that helps knit our students into a family."

What a crock. Apparently, without laptop computers, his students haven't worked together. Now that all his students will tote identical laptop computers, they'll become one happy collaborative family. Suppose he insisted that all business students purchase charcoal gray suits?

Tremendous cultural effects? Requiring a uniform type of computer and a uniform stack of programs will work against those who would prefer to use alternatives. It will marginalize those who would rather work face-to-face than over the screen. For all their talk about bringing students into the real world, educators yearn to place students further into the unreality of cyberspace.

Grant money is notoriously difficult to get, yet somehow it shakes loose more easily for computers than books. Federal, state, and private pilot projects support wiring our schools, distance education, laptop computers, multimedia development, and teacher training. But it's a rare grant that supports teaching clarinet, learning to run a lathe, or stocking a library with new books.

Okay, suppose that you run a school which receives a half-million dollars which can only be spent on computer gear. If you don't use it, the money disappears.

Now suppose that you run a different school which receives a half-million-dollar grant. This one can be spent on anything you wish except electronic gizmos.

Which of those two grants is most likely to be reported in the news? Which will be the more valuable to your school? Which one will most help the students' scholarship, skills, and ultimate maturity? Which will create the more lasting social good?

Few politicians stand up against this school-computer frenzy. As school districts happily dole out money for computers to replace textbooks, they will fix several non-problems, ignore serious and pressing troubles, and create a raft of new headaches.

Multimedia Comics

Weaned on educational games and multimedia encyclopedias, kids naturally seek out the trivial when forced to read real books. While visiting a school librarian, I listened to a high school senior seek help with an assignment: "I'm writing a report about Napoleon," he said. "Can you find me a thin book with lots of pictures?"

Reminds me suspiciously of Classics Illustrated—comic books based on great literature. Forty years ago, a dime would buy a comic book version of *Hamlet, Moby Dick,* or *Huckleberry Finn.*

In a cardboard box that once held bottles of Iroquois beer, I recently discovered my childhood collection of Classics comics. A throwback to when the nation worried that bad comics might corrupt young minds.

My mom, intent on elevating my literary aims from

Scrooge McDuck to Chaucer, gave me a subscription to Classics Illustrated for my twelfth birthday. Every few weeks, *The Three Musketeers* or *Two Years Before the Mast* would sweep me away to centuries past. Curled up next to the lukewarm radiator, I'd fight off predatory sisters and escape with "Thrilling, Exciting, Romantic Adventure stories, endorsed by Educators."

On the cover of *The Octopus,* a cowboy's shooting a charging railroad engine. The next month's issue showed a caped Macbeth gazing at a floating dagger. A few weeks later, the postman brought Mark Twain's *Pudd'nhead Wilson,* introduced with a tense pistol duel.

Educational? Uh, maybe. My mom's efforts were diluted by the mix of comics I'd get my hands on. I'd read an abbreviated version of *Ivanhoe,* then grab the latest adventures of Superman and dream of a cool Jimmy Olsen radio-wristwatch. At best, an ambivalent introduction to great literature.

Those Classics comics were a stepping-stone on the path leading through Cliff's Notes to the promised land of the *Reader's Digest.* Written with the noble goal of educating, entertaining, and enhancing childhood experiences, they succeeded. At the same time, they failed.

Each volume concluded with the token line "Now that you have read the Classics Illustrated edition, don't miss the added enjoyment of reading the original, obtainable at your school or public library." Yeah. How many kids put down their comic books and headed to the library? Even today, all I know of *Silas Marner* is whatever an anonymous hack circled in George Eliot's novel.

Yet these comics gave me the comforting feeling that great literature actually was intelligible. And a sense of confidence that when I grew up, I might be able to read—possibly even understand—*Jane Eyre.* Later, when my college English prof assigned the real stories, they had a vague familiarity, as if I'd experienced a mental prologue. Somehow I retained a tad . . . as if I'd met Mr. Rochester before and knew he was a good guy.

Today, as I sit in the attic rereading those Classics comics, I'm still ambivalent. The drawings do bring the text alive. But instead of nourishing my imagination, I'm spoon-fed some artist's image of Hamlet . . . one that's as flat as the condensed story line. Like Campbell's Cream of Broccoli, they deliver an institutionalized interpretation of nourishment.

Without knowing it, my tastes have been shaped by a diet of canned vegetables. It reminds me of why classical music lovers can't forgive Walt Disney. Whenever they hear Beethoven's Pastorale Symphony, their imagination runs off to topless female centaurs with neither belly buttons nor nipples.

The comic book version includes this disclaimer: "Because of space limitations, we regretfully omitted some of the original characters and sub-plots of this novel. Nevertheless, we have retained its main theme and mood . . ."

Not that I can do much better—how do you squeeze *Crime and Punishment* into a fifty-page comic book? It's the limitation of the medium: They deliver simple cartoon images. The text is secondary.

Flipping through these old comic books, I'm struck by their resemblance to today's educational multimedia. Dialogue gets condensed, soliloquies abbreviated, characters dropped. The main element on each page is pictures; words are inserted almost as a second thought.

But the Internet hasn't the space limitations that confront comic books. So why don't we find better storytelling on-line?

Well, for one thing, you can't tell a story with hypertext. The very format of the Web works against it. Hypertext doesn't allow narrative: Depending on which hot link you pick, the tale takes a different turn. It turns a story into a computer game.

On the Web, storytelling gets undercut in another way. Using hypertext, the programmer doesn't know where a reader came from. So every page on the Web has to stand on its own, independent of every other page. How do you develop a plot when it's difficult to read the text from beginning to end?

As a result, the Web trivializes text. With only a second to catch the reader's eye, the Internet emphasizes flashy graphics and bright colors. Any text is there to support the graphic, resulting in short paragraphs that closely resemble captions. Just like comic books.

Authors become graphics designers and caption writers when they write for the Web. In literature, the text is primary. On the Web, words just get in the way.

Same's true with multimedia encyclopedias. They're typically packaged free with the purchase of a home computer, allowing parents to think that the computer they've just bought is somehow educational. But these software encyclopedias, so rich with pictures, have almost no depth. If Classics Illustrated ever had the chutzpah to condense an encyclopedia

into a comic book, they'd make a CD-ROM multimedia encyclopedia.

Paul Roberts writes multimedia essays to be published on
educational CD-ROMs. It's a good job, he reports in the June
1996 issue of *Harper's Magazine*. Easy work, good pay, comfortable
workplace. There's just one problem: Multimedia doesn't satisfy
that writer.

"The irony of the information revolution is that consumers
neither like nor expect long, densely written texts on their
computer screens. Long texts addle the eyes; they slow the
rapid-fire 'interactive' process, steal precious screen space from
the animation, video, and multimedia's other, more marketable
gewgaws."

Of thousands of essays that Mr. Roberts has written, perhaps forty are longer than two hundred words. Most are a
paragraph long. Before electronic media, he regularly wrote
deeply researched articles about the environment. "Nowadays
whole months go by when I do nothing but crank out info-
nuggets on whatever topics the multimedia companies believe
will sell well . . . It is, without question, hack writing, the
kind of pap (I used to think) only the feckless and unprincipled
had the nerve or need to take."

It has to be this way. The author of any Web page doesn't
know who the reader is or where she came from. Every multimedia entry stands alone . . . it can't be tied to the next
page, since the viewer might jump somewhere else. That's how
you write captions for pictures—assume that the reader just
stumbled onto the picture, then give the shortest possible sum-

mary of the graphic. No room for elaboration, subtlety, or ambivalence.

Unlike a newspaper or book, multimedia discourages the caption reader from entering the text. It's painful to read any long text on a computer screen. After a few pages, your eyes glaze over and your fingers nervously reach for the mouse. A click refreshes the screen with a completely different image. And so, postmodern, non-linear hypertext replaces old-fashioned storytelling.

Whether a multimedia encyclopedia or an electronic teaching system, animation sells the product, not storytelling and certainly not quality research.

As Paul Roberts points out, multimedia writers "needn't be experts so much as filters whose task is to absorb and compress great gobs of information into small, easily digestible on-screen chunks. Brevity and blandness: These are the elements of the next literary style.

"What depresses me most about multimedia writing is its sheer pleasurelessness. Multimedia writing is not about telling a story. It's about telling fragments of stories, fragments that may or may not add up to anything. At the end of the project, you're left saturated and unfulfilled, ready to burst."

Just as multimedia turns writers into hacks, it likewise stifles readers. The computer pushes us to fool around instead of digging for meaning in the text. Like paging through a *Life* magazine, we focus on the pretty pictures, occasionally glancing at the text.

On the other hand, Classics Illustrated didn't do obvious damage. Those comic books didn't prevent me from reading the real thing, even though they gave me the feeling that I didn't have to. And, indeed, the condensed stories actually followed the originals: Macbeth does get killed in the end. Maybe the measure of a great book is its ability to be watered down and still hold the reader's attention.

This much: No promoter of Classics Illustrated ever suggested that putting great literature into comics would foment a renaissance in literature. Nobody who condensed *Huckleberry Finn* into a comic book would claim that it's a revolutionary way to learn. No aspiring writer ever yearned to put his best work into Classics comics.

Me? After reading my abbreviated version of *The House of the Seven Gables,* I'm off the bookstore. I've seen the thin book with lots of pictures. I'm ready for the real thing.

CRTs for Tots

At what age should children start using computers? According to Knowledge Adventure Company, nine-month-olds can benefit from computers. Their consultant, Corinne Rupert, says that their software will "give them a comfort level with computers." So Knowledge Adventure now sells Jump Start Baby, a program aimed at pre-toddlers nine to twenty-four months old.

If you think it's bizarre to start infants on computers, stop by some high-tech nurseries and day-care centers. ComputerTots teaches computing to kids from three years old upward; CompuChild franchisees visit nurseries, teaching computing to two-year-olds. With music, color graphics, animation, and the CompuPal Pedro, they claim their "fun-filled classes are educational and entertaining and provide PreSchoolers with a 'jump-start' on the computerized world of today and tomorrow."

Is computing so difficult that babies need early childhood training on digital systems? Are computers so essential to life that we should wean two-year-olds on a diet of bleeping animatrons and Teletubbies? Exactly why do infants need "a comfort level" with computers? Why such an emphasis on jump-starting into an essentially adult activity, rather than preserving childhood? *

Look—computers aren't tough for children to learn. There's no need to familiarize a baby with a computer in order to prevent computer phobia later on in life. Yes, computers may baffle adults, but children easily adapt to them. Yet our schools latch onto computers as if they're worried that children will—gasp—lapse into book reading and handwriting rather than Web surfing and word processing.

Seymour Papert of the MIT Media Lab has a deeper—and creepier—agenda. He foresees the day when the converged computer-television will provide communications, education, enrichment, and entertainment. Instead of distrusting the computer as a device which isolates us from each other, families should revel in technological togetherness: Parents can keep diaries of their own Internet activities, and compare them with their kids' activities. A child who likes turtles might receive a birthday present of a specially created World Wide Web directory with plenty of turtle pictures; in return, she'll pass along a list of favorite Internet sites to Grandma. Enriched, eh?

Papert sees that soon, technology will be the center of both

* How come we avoid jump-starting cars, yet want to jump-start children? Aren't kids the perfect example of self-starters?

school and home. Soon after birth, infants will receive computers—pleasantly disguised as cute stuffed animals—ready to respond as the newborn touches, hits, or gurgles at it. Papert wants to give computers to children who are just learning to talk, if only to let them generate geometric shapes. (Of course, his wishes are already coming true—cuddly dolls for infants come equipped with embedded computers, complete with synthesized speech.)

Rather than parents worrying about their kids spending too many hours behind the cathode-ray tube, Papert says that the folks should join in. Find out more about computers by spending lots of time on the net. Communicate with your children over two-way video. Celebrate when your children spend nights on-line. It's never too early to begin.

Make you feel queasy? Me too. Sounds like B. F. Skinner's novel *Walden Two,* where the clay of youth is molded into the perfect society of the future. Skinner would have loved to see infants and pre-schoolers snuggling up to warm, fuzzy pre-programmed computers.

Watch pre-schoolers play on a computer. They seem to confirm Skinner's behavioristic experiments: Five-year-olds quickly advance through Math Blaster shooting down UFOs. Not entirely unlike pigeons trained to work for rewards. Doubtless, we're conditioning our kids for careers as video arcade professionals—or perhaps airport flight controllers?

Children easily learn the logic built into programs. They're good at figuring out software. This has so impressed Seymour Papert that he's built an entire teaching system around it. But the dry, predictable logic of computers—whether embedded in Myst, Logo, or Nintendo—is utterly unlike the logic of dealing with other children. Great preparation for a world of Boolean algebra; an utterly inadequate introduction to a life dealing with people.

Computers deliver an abundance of symbols yet offer an improverishment of experience. Do our children need to see more icons, corporate logos, and glitzy fonts . . . or do they need more time climbing, running, and figuring out how to get along with each other?

Child psychologist Jane Healy writes, "Putting normally developing babies on computers for any length of time is so ridiculous that it hardly bears any further comment." Dr. Healy points to animal research looking at augmented sensory experience and abnormal overstimulation. These studies have shown lasting negative effects on attention and learning. Scientists, of course, can't ethically perform such experiments on humans. But plenty of day-care centers do—devout believers in high-tech blather. Our first few years are of utmost importance in developing motor dexterity and emotional attachment. These are some of the very skills blunted by excessive time on computers.

In Silicon Valley, two-income parents typically send their pre-schoolers to day-care centers, where the children are plopped before CRT and keyboard. By the time they're in kindergarten, many kids have spent hundreds of hours on computers.

When Robert and Shelly Young moved to Los Altos, California, with their six-year-old son, they didn't worry about him fitting into the high-powered elementary school; after all, he had flourished during his year in a rural kindergarten. A month into classes, the first-grade teacher takes the Youngs aside and tells them sternly, "Your son needs tutoring because he's far behind the others." The parents swallow hard and ask, "In what subject?" The teacher replies, in complete seriousness, "Keyboarding."

Some nursery schools broadcast live images over the Internet, so parents can watch their children via the World Wide Web. It's Big Brother over the net. Pretty soon, toddlers will be equipped with pagers and cell phones. A connected family? Perhaps. But hardly together.

Of course, the price of classroom computers isn't simply the cost of the gizmos. In Columbus, Ohio, Dana Elementary School installed three Compaq Presario computers in their kindergarten, despite the kindergarten teacher telling the principal that computers were superfluous. Nevertheless, the technicians lugged in the equipment, and hauled out the sandbox and block table. There wasn't enough room.

Computers aren't compatible with the clay, dirt, and cookie dust of a five-year-old's life. Kids mustn't pour sand into the keyboard or smear peanut butter on the monitor—tough rules to enforce in a kindergarten. I met a second-grade teacher who discarded the magnets from her classroom because she feared they would erase the floppy disks. Her students now learn about magnetism from some multimedia program.

Ellen Specter has taught kindergarten in Cherry Hill, New Jersey, for thirty-two years. She's seen a sharp drop in children's creativity, attributing part of that to computers: "They expect the visual image to come up before them," Mrs. Specter said. "Everything is instant. They don't have to play. When you ask them to color whatever they want, many will say, 'I don't know what to color.' "

The computer changes the ecology of the classroom. Predictably, kids love the new computers and the kindergarten increasingly looks and sounds like a video arcade. Meanwhile, the machine becomes the center of attention, pushing aside clay, crayon, and teacher. Kids fight over access, with the boys seeming to always get first crack. Questions change from "Why are there wrinkles on your face?" to "Why won't he let me play on the computer?"

Somehow, computers are supposed to be "good" because they're interactive and non-commercial. Television is "bad" because it's passive and commercial. Videotapes, on the whole, are "good" because they don't have commercials. I'll bet that to a child, there's not much difference. All provide big, colorful cathode-ray tubes. All show their favorite characters in fast-paced animated clips. All deliver long stretches of mental excitement with minimal muscular activity.

Suppose we wanted to encourage attention deficit syndrome. I can't think of a better way than to point youngsters at fast animated video clips. Give 'em electronic games with races, spaceship dogfights, shoot-'em-ups, and lots of explosive noises, garish colors, and disconnected information coming from diverse sources. Give them post-modern hyper-linked media rather than simple storytelling. Encourage them to write programs with computerized Turtle Graphics rather than touching a real turtle. In short, lock them in an electronic classroom.

Doubtless, multimedia systems provide visually stimulating images. Almost every children's software product is labeled "exciting." But lack of excitement simply isn't a genuine problem for kids. If anything, they're exposed to too many animated screens, with TV, videos, and Nintendo. Show me the computer program that encourages quiet reflection.

Do computers stimulate curiosity? Well, if curiosity means wondering about the effect of clicking on a mysterious screen icon, then yes, computers certainly encourage a certain kind of sterile curiosity. But if curiosity means wondering what happens when you mix clay with sand or if rubber bands can be frozen—the experience of real life—well, computers have nothing to do with it.

What happens when you set a pre-schooler behind a computer paint program? The graphics software will teach her how to manipulate a mouse, how to select from menus, and how to fill in geometric shapes. She'll also learn to wait her turn at the keyboard—after all, the computer is a one-kid-at-a-time experience.

Now give the kid some fingerpaints and a sheet of butcher paper. It's slimy, gooey, messy. Paints smear, dribble, and drip. The colors mix unpredictably. She learns to practice using her arms and fingers. She'll make handprints. Figure out the effects of a brush. How to mix colors. And to make it a collaborative effort, just add more kids.

That computer graphics program is perfect for pre-school

warehouses for children. It's neat and self-contained. No need for washcloths, no spills on the floor, and nothing to clean up. Moreover, computers isolate children from each other, making the kids easier to handle.

Plenty of computer programs have strong educational content with minimal computer glitz. Yet the medium broadcasts a powerful message: We're training the youngest children to explore through a computer rather than with their hands, feet, and imagination.

The World Wide Web can bring hundreds of images of whales and dolphins—much more impressive-looking than the handful of goldfish in a typical pre-school's fishbowl. Oh, but those fish mean more to a child than any images of the computer. They're not just pictures. They're alive.

Look at the refrigerator of any family with pre-schoolers: Under the magnets, you'll find newsprint colored with Crayolas. Parents value the hand-drawn and homemade, no matter how crude. My own two kids find the best part of a new computer is the shipping container: Monitors come in big, strong boxes, easily carved up to make playhouses, caves, and boats.

I can hardly think of a less appropriate place to put computers than kindergartens and pre-schools. Think of the things a three-year-old most needs: love, affection, personal attention, human warmth, and mainly, care. Four- and five-year-olds need to develop human skills . . . how to get along with others. They should be playing with things, not images.

Yet you'll find computers in most every kindergarten. Go figure.

A Question of Balance

Whenever challenged about bringing computers into children's lives, technologists respond that, of course, we need balance. In his book *The Connected Family,* Seymour Papert writes glowingly about the great benefits of computers to our children (focusing especially on the software which he's written). He disarms any criticism by saying that balance is everything. You must set a balance for children between reading, playing music, watching movies, and television.

So where is that wonderful balance point? For some things, the best balance for children is zero. Alcohol, for example. Cigarettes. Street drugs. What's the right balance of violent images? For other things, the best balance may be as much as possible . . . say, parental attention.

How much is a balanced amount of television? In the first

edition of *Baby and Child Care,* Benjamin Spock advised, "In general, if a child is taking care of his homework, staying outside with his friends in the afternoon, coming to supper, going to bed when it's time, and not being frightened, I would be inclined to let him spend as much of his evening with television or radio as he chooses." Hey—this was back in the late 1940s, when TV was a wonderland of promise. After a few years of seeing television's effects, Dr. Spock changed his mind. Later versions of his book read, "The hours for watching television should be limited . . ."

It is possible to watch too little television? Well, I've met a few five-year-olds who have never watched television. They're doing great: pretty much like other kids entering kindergarten, except they're refreshingly innocent, and surprisingly non-violent. According to several studies, these children have longer attention spans, too. Perhaps the best balance of television in a pre-school child's life is as little as possible. Yet I'll bet the Teletubbies producers argue otherwise.

Okay, what's the right amount of computing for a six-year-old kid? Certainly, that child doesn't need a computer to do research in kindergarten, nor to write compositions. No pressing need to send e-mail, check into chat rooms, or download updates. Besides entertainment, about all the machine does is teach the kid how to fool with a computer. So why did the Santa Cruz Public School System install four computers in each kindergarten?

"To make our children comfortable with computers" comes the reply from one school administrator. "When children grow up around computers, they won't be afraid of them later on." A nice theory, but fear of computers simply isn't a problem confronting our youth.

I'm not advocating zero computers for children, nor do I propose heaving out the electronic gizmos cluttering our classrooms. Indeed, there are a million ways to balance human concerns with machine interactions, and each of us will make our own choice. My point is that it's possible to do perfectly well without any computers or high-tech teaching devices. For many—children and adults alike—zero computing is perfectly acceptable and even singularly desirable. How can a school achieve such a balance?

This quest for balance reminds me of balancing on an I beam on the roof of the Concrete Central elevator in Lackawanna, New York. It's the seventh stupidest thing I ever did.

Back in the 1900s, when Midwest wheat was milled in the East, Great Lakes freighters shipped tons of grain into Buffalo harbor. Stored there in a huge wooden warehouse, the wheat would be ground into cereal over the winter. Worked fine, although the wooden buildings had a few problems.

Like explosions. Chaff and dust from dry wheat made for spectacular blasts; one morning in 1887, a whole block of nearby warehouses disappeared with a convulsive roar heard for miles. Remember, this was in the days of gaslights and steam engines, and it took only a spark to set off the elevator's dust-laden atmosphere.

Enter concrete. Along a Minneapolis railroad track, Max Toltz built the first concrete elevator in 1899. It worked so well that by 1917, A. E. Baxter created the huge Concrete Central with some two hundred cylinders of storage. Worked fine, until the 1950s when the milling industry moved out of my hometown, leaving behind an unused port and warnings from school principals never to go near the abandoned grain elevators.

Returning home after finishing grad school, I began to wonder: Why is there such a conspiracy to keep us out of grain elevators? What secret do they hold? I figured that the invulnerability granted by my recently awarded Ph.D. would allow me to balance my professional responsibilities as an astronomer with a non-professional irresponsibility to undertake a quest. A search for the ultimate truth. To uncover the great mystic Cabala that must be hidden at the apex of the city's grain elevator.

So I set out with one other idiot to explore this long-abandoned grain elevator. Seems they don't build grain elevators in residential neighborhoods: The roads have long been weeded over and there's nobody near. We're maybe a mile from downtown, yet hiking through utter urban isolation: no electricity, no phones, no roads, nothing but a huge concrete elevator. Break your leg in this desolation, and you'll be discovered in a few years. Maybe.

Apparently to discourage morons from entering, the city fathers demolished the first two levels of the staircase. Their efforts force us to snag a climbing rope around a beam and enter through a broken window on the elevator's exoskeleton.

Inside, the spalled concrete shows rusty reinforcing bars

twisting through the walls. It's the skeleton of America's great industrial era.

I feel like an anthropologist, exploring an Egyptian pyramid. On the wall, hieroglyphics tell long-departed souls how to energize now-rusted motors. I half expect to see a concrete engraving, "I am Ozymandias, King of Kings." Instead, graffiti applied with paintbrushes. This must date back to the era before spray paint. Odd—inhabitants of those long-ago times knew the same four-letter words of today's punks.

The rusted staircases work, mostly. A few have collapsed, with serious consequences, were we not equipped with ropes and climbing shoes. After five thousand steps, we reach the top floor, where a sign points to the head-house.

Nifty—at the top of each concrete cylinder, there's a round manhole-sized hole. No cover, no fence, not even a marker. You look down the hole into a Stygian blackness; drop a stone down and you never hear it strike bottom. Dozens of those holes, each leading into a two-hundred-foot concrete pit. No warning signs for this Swiss cheese maze.

Once, a system of conveyor belts carried grain from one elevator cylinder to another—high technology for 1925. Today, the rubberized canvas forms a continuous ribbon of pigeon droppings. Where electrically driven cogs once lifted wheat from lake freighters, there now grows a modest elm tree, rooted several hundred feet above the terrain.

But I'm still not at the top. Two ladders take us up through the ceiling, past a re-election poster for a long-deceased corrupt mayor, and onto the roof. There, the cityscape surrounds us—ships tied to the wharf, cars on the freeway, downtown office buildings—yet we're totally isolated.

An exposed steel I beam connects one section of the roof to the top of the head-house, home of the conveyor belt motors. Balanced on the six-inch-wide beam, I walk across the roof and peer into the apex. There's a one-word message within: "Moxie" For this, I've risked my neck.

Yep, there are safer ways to learn to keep out of abandoned grain elevators. Probably there are whole Web sites devoted to warning us to stay away from those firetraps. Which reminds me of the need for balance in the classroom.

A balance of technology and human interaction might have prevented me from wasting a Saturday and almost getting killed. Maybe I'd have been convinced by playing a computer game devoted to showing kids getting squashed in grain silos. Maybe. But somehow, I doubt it.

Come to think of it, that's true of all the stupid things I've done in my life: No warning on any computer screen would have prevented me from going right ahead. Balance? Bah.

Calculating Against
Calculators

ow could anyone argue against bringing computers into a mathematics class? After all, computers are natural number crunchers. Wherever you find algebra, equations, and logic, there's a computer. Of all places that computers belong, shouldn't it be math class?

Well, no.

The computer and its kid brother, the hand calculator, work against learning basic arithmetic. They work against appreciating the nature of math. Against familiarity with numbers. Against acquiring an understanding of algebra.

Thanks to digital electronics, students get answers without manipulating concepts: Problem solving becomes button-pressing. It's not necessary to understand how to formulate abstract quantities. Rather, you go straight from numbers to answers. Calculators deliver answers with minimum thought. Confronted by a numeric problem, students naturally reach for electronics, rather than experience. The device first adopted to strengthen mathematical understanding has become a crutch which hobbles the development of numeric literacy.

You no longer need to memorize the times tables to multiply. No surprise that students weaned on calculators can't multiply in their heads. They can't divide. They're minimally cognizant of basic arithmetic.

Watch kids solve math problems with a calculator: They punch the buttons, see the result, and accept what the machine tells 'em. A geography student hands in an assignment where she calculates the height of a Toronto broadcast tower as 0.0034117 millimeters. Numerical literacy tells us to question each result, but the authority of the calculator dulls our critical sense.

Today's students receive only passing exposure to arithmetic tables.* Burned into every calculator, these tables are fundamental to all numeric understanding. Without knowing how to add and multiply, you can't tell when you're being rooked.

Sad to say, learning to multiply isn't a feel-good project, so beloved of the self-esteem movement. Rather, learning the times tables requires rote drill work. It's not fun, like shooting down Martians on a computer screen. But it's one of those must-learn-or-else lessons, without which you're eliminated from many fields of human endeavor.

---

* Also true for handwriting. Penmanship, spelling, and grammar aren't considered worthy of instruction, so they're pushed aside for word processing. Result: Surprisingly few high school students can write clearly.

Kids once had to learn basic arithmetic in second grade. This was back when you often confronted numbers: making change, tipping a waitress, recognizing bargains, balancing checkbooks, understanding public expenditures.

Hey—those demands haven't disappeared. Today there are more numbers in our life than fifty years ago. We're confronted with sales tax, toll roads, discounts, balloon mortgages, and state lotteries. Indeed, our economic and scientific worlds demand more—not less—familiarity with math.

"Thanks to calculators, we get through arithmetic fast," educators tell me. "Children can then advance quickly to more advanced topics. There's so much to learn in math that we shouldn't waste time on the arithmetic tables."

This, of course, is backward. You gotta learn basics before progressing to advanced topics. Without a firm grounding in arithmetic, you'll drown when you hit the high-power stuff. Calculators and computers short-circuit the stepwise progression in learning. Shall we teach reading without requiring children to tediously memorize the alphabet?

Most students won't continue on to higher math. For them, the most important thing they can learn in math is basic arithmetic . . . the kind of math that lets you make change and balance your checkbook. These students get cheated when they're taught to solve the problem on the calculator.

Yep, lots of kids trip over arithmetic and algebra. This is the very reason why we should emphasize these areas and spend more time on them. It's why we shouldn't hand out calculators.

Mathematician Neal Koblitz tells of playing math games with sixth graders at Seattle's Washington Middle School. To explore rounding off, they'd divide numbers by seven and give the answer to the nearest integer. What's sixty divided by seven? Good answers include "About nine" or "A little more than eight." But the calculator-equipped kids got 8.5714285 . . . and couldn't interpret the answer. They read out numbers, but didn't understand the decimal point.

Moreover, those blinking digits obscure deeper truths. The circumference of a circle isn't 3.14159 times its diameter, but rather π times the diameter. And how do you grade a student who says that two thirds times three is 1.9999999?

Getting around in life depends on ballpark estimates, approximations, and rounding off. These become second nature after you know manual arithmetic . . . after all, they're mental shortcuts. But if you've always depended on a calculator, well, good luck figuring a 20 percent tip. Don't ask that teenager at the checkout counter—she probably can't make change without a cash register.

Math educators, discouraged by centuries of bad feelings directed at their profession, have long searched for new ways to teach math. I was the victim of one of these evangelical movements: the New Math.

Back in the 1960s, when smart foreigners threatened America, modern educators invented the New Math. And Buffalo's Millard Fillmore Junior High School was modern. We wouldn't study some old-fashioned algebra. We'd learn the latest: set theory, Venn diagrams, and number bases.

After three years of New Math, I knew all about the communicative law of addition and the union of sets. I could multiply in base seven. And I could write the symbol for the null set—the collection of nothingness.

So I start high school without knowing algebra. My chemistry teacher writes an equation on the board. A's and B's and C's . . . and they all add up to zero. Here I am, budding science jock, and I can't balance a chemistry equation. I'm sweating blood, looking for something to hang a solution on. But there's nothing about set theory or number bases. Just letters dancing on the chalkboard. And a most unwelcome equal sign.

Thanks to the New Math, I knew lots of squiggly symbols but hardly ever saw an equal sign. Algebra—so essential to science—had to be learned outside of math class. I wasn't taught how to solve equations, but I sure knew that the null set was a collection of nothingness.

The null set pretty much sums up the New Math. Within two decades, it was recognized as an utter flop. But not before a generation of college-bound students—smart and stupid alike—dutifully learned all about theoretical laws of multiplication. By 1975, the New Math collapsed like a punctured whoopee cushion.

But if you think the New Math was idiotic, you haven't heard of the New New Math. It goes under the names of Complete Math, Connected Math, Reform Math, Constructivist Math, or Fuzzy Math. It all adds up to Mickey Mouse Math.

Instead of teaching arithmetic and algebra, students get a half-baked casserole of "real-world problems" to be taught through "discovery learning" and solved by "group work." Lu-cille Renwick, who covers education for the *Los Angeles Times,* reports how New New Math handles a problem in two-digit arithmetic: Children "would join together in groups and dis-cuss how many beans or sticks it takes to make 10 . . . They'd collect the tens and then discuss the ones. The students would work out the problem until they understood tens and ones. Reaching an answer would not be paramount."

This isn't math. At best, it's math appreciation, And the result of group work isn't understanding. Perhaps you wind up with a bunch of kids who are good at splitting up work and copying answers. Most likely, a few kids will do most of the work and several confused onlookers try to follow along. But everyone gets an A.

The New New Math is promoted by the National Council of Teachers of Mathematics, joined by the National Science Foun-dation. They recommend "the integration of the calculator into the school mathematics program at all grade levels in class work, homework and evaluation" and that "every mathematics teacher at every level promote the use of calculators." They justify this with feel-good mumbo jumbo: "The cognitive gain in number sense, conceptual development, and visualization can empower and motivate students to engage in true mathe-matical problem solving."

Learning algebra in eighth grade is a key to success in col-lege. Yet school boards hate to inflict rigorous courses on un-willing students. They advertise rigorous algebra, but deliver a vapid curriculum, with a heavy emphasis on computing. The natural effect is a continual dumbing down of both curriculum and graduates.

In the heart of Silicon Valley, Palo Alto's school board has provided a decade of New New Math, along with a heavy dose of computers. In 1996 they polled parents only to discover a deep dissatisfaction over the number of math facts and techniques the children were learning. Depending on grade, between half and two thirds of families reported hiring outside tutors for their children.

Palo Alto parents, among the nation's wealthiest and best educated, can often afford after-school programs and private math tutors. Other parents have a rougher time when their schools latch onto these touchy-feely math programs.

Arizona State University Professor Marianne Jennings noticed that her daughter Sarah had received an A in high school algebra, yet couldn't solve an equation. Sarah's textbook, *Secondary Math: An Integrated Approach, Focus on Algebra,* includes photos of Mali wood carvings, Maya Angelou's poetry, and praise for the wife of Pythagoras. Questions posed to students include "What role should zoos play in our society?"

It's Rain-Forest Math according to Dr. Jennings. Despite the book's title, algebra isn't actually being taught. Sarah's class would measure their wingspans one day; the next they'd toss coins all period. Showing their work on homework or tests was optional. Rather than learning math, children were taught mathematical concepts.

Mathematical concepts? Yale's Professor David Gelernter writes, "Most people have no use for 'mathematical concepts' anyway—arithmetic yes, group theory no. For the others, the theory that 'real math' has nothing to do with arithmetic is wrong—engineers and hard scientists are invariably intimate with numbers. They have to be. So if you don't go on in math, basic arithmetic is crucial. Whereas if you do go on in math, basic arithmetic is crucial."

Dr. Jennings naturally spoke with Sarah's math teacher, only to hear that "We don't plug and chug anymore. We're teaching them to think." Outraged by this justification of academic pablum, she approached the school administrators. Ultimately, a school board member told her, "You may just have to face the fact that your daughter won't get algebra." Whee!

Professor Gelernter writes, "The yawning chasm between ed-school doctrine and common sense has already swallowed up (to our national shame) a whole generation of American kids. Big reforms are needed, but the electronic calculator perfectly captures what the struggle is about. When you hand children an automatic, know-it-all crib sheet, you undermine learning—obviously. So let's get rid of the damned things. Professional educators are leading us full-speed toward a world of smart machines and stupid people."

Practice—repeated drill—is out of favor today . . . witness that Arizona math instructor's scorn for "plug and chug." Yet it's the core of math competency. If we want students that can handle math, they've got to memorize the times tables. Do plenty of problem sets. Master algebra . . . don't just talk about it in vague, fuzzy terms.

"Don't forget that computer programming teaches students

to think," says a friend of mine who's a computer jock in Silicon Valley. He's deeply invested in technology and has no kids. "Programming is a logical system that rewards clear reasoning."

Uh, sure. Nineteenth-century schoolmasters used the same reasoning to justify teaching ancient languages. According to computer scientist Joseph Weizenbaum, "There is, as far as I know, no more evidence that programming is good for the mind than that Latin is."

Anyway, programming teaches us to think of problems as solvable through the sterile Boolean logic of AND, OR, NOT, and IF. Snaggly real-world problems require common sense, buttressed by familiarity with numbers. The ability to construct an argument and spot logical fallacies has little to do with creating computer codes.

Then, too, calculators and computers trivialize mistakes. When he gets a wrong answer, a student will typically dismiss the mistake with "Oh, I just pressed the wrong button!" rather than recognizing that he went about solving a problem the wrong way.

Good algebra teachers demand that students show their work to see whether a mistake's due to calculation or misunderstanding. You got a good grade if you took a good path to the answer but made a mistake in calculation. Students were graded on the method, not just the final answer. But when a calculator's in use, there's no trail of reasoning and no telling why a mistake occurred, so the instructor can't tell the difference.

The Educational Testing Service, purveyors of standardized tests like the SAT and GRE, compared fourth- and eighth-grade students who used computers to learn math. Analyzing a 1996 survey, Harold Wenglinsky found that when eighth graders used computers mainly for math drills like dividing fractions, test scores averaged half a grade lower than for other students.

Mr. Wenglinsky reports that for both fourth and eighth graders, "The frequency of school computer use was negatively related to academic achievement."

Those who used computer programs that encouraged "higher-level cognitive practices" scored slightly higher than those who did not. Similarly, fourth graders who used interactive math games scored slightly higher than those who used the computers mainly for math drills.

His survey showed that a teacher's computing competence has the most effect on whether technology helped or hindered the students. Mr. Wenglinsky concludes that schools should insist on teacher training in technology. But his survey shows that over three fourths of all teachers have already taken specialized professional classes in how to use technology—that's pretty close to saturation. Teaching more computing to teachers isn't going to make better students.

Look: Teachers should teach . . . not become computer jocks. When educational films were the rage, plenty of teachers had to learn how to thread movie projectors. We didn't send them to summer schools for projectionists. Who'll make the better math teacher: the guy that loves math and wants to tell you his latest topology adventures, or the propellerhead who can surf the Web and is an expert at downloading files?

Samuel Sava, executive director of the National Association of Elementary School Principals, writes that "37 percent of students used computers in at least some math lessons. Yet this increased use seems to make no difference to our math results. In sum, if computers make a difference, it has yet to show up in achievement."

Even in college, computers work against mathematical competence. Calculus professors have long been frustrated by high dropout rates. Sad to say, calculus, like much of math, is tough. But it's essential throughout engineering and science . . . it's the common language of the physical sciences.

So the University of Illinois developed a calculus course centered on the computer program Mathematica. This software neatly solves problems in arithmetic, algebra, trigonometry, and calculus. Instead of teaching how to integrate functions, instructors teach how to integrate using Mathematica.

Predictably, college students learn how to run the Mathematica program, but they don't learn calculus. Adam Eyring, studying environmental sciences and engineering at the University of North Carolina at Chapel Hill, felt his course was a disaster because "it was hard to go from a program that does your computations for you to doing it by hand."

Professor Jonathan Reichert has taught college physics for some thirty years. His advanced undergraduates learn about nuclear magnetic resonance by flipping spinning electrons in magnetic fields. "The data collection part isn't challenging stuff," Dr. Reichert says. "After the kids set up the experiment, they read off points on an oscilloscope, take the log of the number, then plot the data on a graph. You've got to plot the data as you take it, so that you can uncover your mistakes, root out systematic errors, and keep the apparatus working right. By plotting the answers by hand, crazy answers pop out right away."

But for the past three or four years, students refuse to plot the data as they collect it. Instead they write down the data, take it home, and draw the graphs on their computers. It wastes time, since their first graphs inevitably show a problem that they could have quickly uncovered in the lab.

"They want automatic answers," observes Dr. Reichert, shaking his head. "Students can't stand the manual labor of drawing simple graphs. Or maybe they no longer know how. Either way, they miss out on what it means to do physics."

Now I know Professor Reichert—twenty-five years ago, he taught me the physics of electricity and magnetism. Right after his section on circuit analysis, he stops me in the hallway and hands me six electronic resistors. "What happens if you connect twelve 100 ohm resistors into a cube, with a single resistor on each edge?" he challenges me. "What'll be the resistance across the opposite corners?"

I roll the problem around in my mind, knowing that there's got to be an easy way to answer this question. But it's hairy— when I draw the schematic, some resistors are in series, others in parallel. I can't see a simple way to analyze this circuit. It's not obvious whether the answer will be more or less than a hundred ohms.

What to do? Well, I get out the soldering gun, clip leads, and ohmmeter. Damn, but it's about 83 ohms. How come? I don't know why, but that's what the meter says. Next day, without blinking I tell Dr. Reichert the answer. He won't let me off the hook. Wants to know how I got it. I show him my carefully constructed cube of resistors, and he rolls his eyes.

I'd cheated—or at least taken a shortcut. Instead of recognizing a chance to apply what I should have learned in physics, I reached for the soldering gun. Today, students would fire up the SPICE electronic circuit analysis software to get the answer to six digits of precision, yet still not understand Ohm's law, Kirchoff's law, and how to deal with resistors in series and parallel.

Ironically, Professor Reichert notes that today, the one area of computing that's hardly ever taught is data collection. "Students don't mind fooling with pretty software, but they're lost if you ask them to wire up a computer to control an experiment.

"Hey, I love teaching physics and I've paid my dues on computers," he says. "If the computer's such a wonderful learning tool, show me the evidence that our students are better prepared. Even though they're constantly in contact with electronic devices, they certainly don't know much electronics. They don't know how to assemble and manage even simple experiments. The best students that come through here are the immigrants whose parents can't afford computers."

Mathematician Neal Koblitz believes that computers are unnecessary in the study of mathematics from kindergarten through college calculus. He writes that computers in schools drain resources, corrupt educators, work for bad pedagogy, and hold a broad anti-intellectual appeal.

The drain of resources is obvious, as is the corruption of educators (who do you think sponsors all the Computers in Education conferences?). The bad pedagogy shows up in television shows about math and science, such as the public television show "Square One." It's heavy on gimmickry and pays little attention to content. This ambiance carries into computer software as well: Program developers work hard on graphics and sounds, and only rarely consult with teachers.

That anti-intellectual appeal of the Internet? Look at the many popular World Wide Web pages which ridicule learning, knowledge, tradition, authority, and scholarship. Dr. Miles Everett wrote about television but his words could equally apply to much of what crosses the Internet: "Its methods, pace, and style constantly denigrate the values essential in schooling, concentration, disciplined analysis, wrestling with complexity, and pursuit of understanding."

Larry Braden has received the presidential award for excellence in teaching. You'll find him in front of the chalkboard at St. Paul's School in Concord, New Hampshire. It's one of those old private schools, charging tens of thousands a year. No shortage of good students.

"I've been teaching math for thirty years," he says. "But much as I love computers and enjoy working through algorithms, I sense that computers are ruining math education. Math is a deductive endeavor and computers substitute punching numbers for understanding concepts.

"On the computer, anyone can program the quadratic formula," Larry tells me. "You hit the coefficients a, b, and c, then voilà, there are the roots. With the answer on the computer's screen, you think that you know math. But you don't."

I'm chatting with Larry—he looks a bit like Mr. Chips—when he looks up and asks point-blank: "What's the average speed of the earth around the sun?"

"I ask every entering student this question," he continues. "Twenty years ago, three quarters of 'em could solve it. Now, it's maybe one in three."

I scramble for a second and suddenly realize that Larry's not asking an astronomy question so much as a simple math problem. High school kids know that the earth goes around the sun once a year. At least they ought to. They know the distance from sun to earth—again, they ought to—so apply the formula for a circle.

Plenty of answers: The earth travels some 67,000 miles per hour. Or about 2.5 million kilometers each day. Or 2π astronomical units per year. The main thing isn't getting an exact number. Rather, it's recognizing one more place where the circumference equals π times the diameter.

What's the effect of using computers in math education? Over the past fifteen years, colleges have seen an astounding growth in remedial math classes. Pre-algebra, once the mainstay of seventh and eighth graders, has become a common college class. Indeed, two thirds of college math enrollment is in courses which are ordinarily high school classes.

Math, of course, also means recognizing those problems which simply aren't numerical: If you need two bananas for each loaf of banana bread,* what'll you do with the overripe bunch in your kitchen? Your calculator might tell you to bake three loaves, but common sense might suggest tossing 'em out.

Much of mathematics means translating problems into abstract representations and converting numerical solutions into understanding. It's something that neither calculator nor computer program can do. It's what each of us struggles with whenever we enter the world of numbers. It's why Larry Braden teaches algebra. It's why we'll forever need arithmetic, algebra, and calculus. And it's why computers don't belong in math class.

---

* Mash 2 ripe bananas and mix with 2 eggs, ²/₃ cup sugar, ¹/₃ cup warm butter, 2 cups flour, and 2 teaspoons baking powder. 1¹/₄ hours at 350°F in a 9 × 5 × 3 loaf pan.

Education by E-Mail

Imagine you're a college administrator, worried about declining enrollments and expensive classes. You're competing with nearby colleges. On campus, you're squeezed for classrooms, parking, and dormitory space. The board of directors tells you to reach out into the community. What do you do?

Answer: electronic distance learning.

Imagine you're a professor, assigned to teach a course. You know the material, but you're uncomfortable standing before a classroom. You're pressed for time. You want to spiff up your instruction with multimedia displays. More and more of your students work while attending class. And chalk dust makes you sneeze. Where do you turn?

Answer: electronic distance learning.

Imagine you're working and eager to get promoted. You

need another degree, a credential, or a little more course work, but you can't quit your job to attend college. You want to learn about a subject but it's tough to commute to campus. And you sure can't become a full-time student.

Answer: electronic distance learning.

Seems easy. Like *deus ex machina,* distance learning solves problems for administrator, teacher, and student. How could anyone argue with such an obvious and useful teaching system?

Wait a second. These scenarios address ease of instruction. They assume that learning can somehow be made easy, a process to be shoehorned into an already busy schedule. They don't ask about the quality of an electronic education.

What is electronic distance learning? Typically, a college offers off-campus classes which provide electronically linked instruction. This might include video hookups that send live or pre-taped lectures to your desktop computer. Or the class might be taught in satellite classrooms, where you watch an instructor on a video screen. There may—or may not—be a teacher at the other end of the video hookup.

For some, distance learning may simply mean learning through the Web and exchanging e-mail with an instructor. The central point is that there's no teacher in the room, and the students mainly deal with electronic images.

Distance learning offers all the information, all the facts, all the boredom of an ordinary classroom, with none of the inspiration, none of the commitment, and none of the joy. It's ideal for the student who equates information with education. Perfect for the school that wants to hustle students through with minimal human interaction.

If your view of an education is to learn facts, then just sign up at your local college's Web page. Be sure to bring your credit card.

But if an education is related to skills, experience, and scholarship, then think twice before enrolling in that electronic correspondence school.

Teacher-based learning is social-based: At the end of a semester, you'll know your teacher, and she'll know you. You'll probably also make friends with three other students, dislike one, get along with a few, and not know much about the others.

Distance learning is technology-based. You'll become familiar with e-mail video links, and list servers. By the end of the semester, you may have collaborated with two other students, yet not recognize their faces.

In a distance education course, your instructor may be a hundred miles away. She'll naturally treat you pretty much like an animated face on a video screen . . . the same way that you'll relate to her. She won't know your interests and strengths, won't know your hobbies and abilities. You'll be one more window on her monitor.

How'll you continue your relationship after the semester ends? When it comes time for a letter of recommendation, that instructor will be able to write: "I watched student 72143 on my screen and often exchanged e-mail with him. He will make an excellent android."

Yep, the main purpose of an electronic education is to get a credential, rather than understanding or even recommendations. Distance learning appeals to those who need to maintain a professional license or wish to paper their walls with certificates. It's ideal for the school which wants to award diplomas with a minimum of student-teacher contact. No surprise that distance education is embraced by the University of Phoenix, a leader in adult education.

Advertised as cheap, distance learning can be surprisingly expensive for colleges. When I taught a class at Stanford University, the video linkup required two technicians, seven remotely manipulated cameras, and a roomful of electronics. They need all this gunk to reach perhaps two dozen off-campus students. At the University of California at Berkeley, the campus distance learning center cost several million dollars, plus the ongoing overhead of full-time technicians, administration, equipment upgrading, and video satellite rentals.

What equipment do you need for an ordinary classroom? Desks, chalkboard, and an eraser. The center of the classroom isn't a thing, but a person.

And what pressing problem does the electronic distance learning solve? It mainly offers convenience . . . students don't have to come to a classroom. They needn't immerse themselves in a campus experience.

Certainly, there's a wealth of problems with classical teaching. Boring profs. Lazy students. Inappropriate content. But distance education makes these problems worse. If you think that a teacher is boring, just imagine the same unmotivated guy on a video screen. Won't be long before you hypnotically grab the channel switch.

Distance education promotes the idea that our problems can be solved at a distance. Lowell Monke taught a course in Des Moines where high school students would share their visions of a utopian society with other students around the world. One point of this exercise was to foster a greater understanding of different cultures. The kids loved the course, gleefully exchanging Internet messages with faraway schools.

Yet in the hallway, those same students actively ignored two dozen foreign-born teenagers from some fifteen different nations. The visitors, all studying English as a second language, wanted to converse, but the computer-driven kids didn't. "Learning about other cultures is just a matter of gathering information," Monke said, "but coming to terms with other cultures is not."

Back in 1974, I wrote software to teach planetary astronomy using the Plato Project computers. This was an early nationwide hookup of computers, each with a keyboard, graphics display, and built-in slide projector. The centralized computer handled hundreds of nifty terminals located at campuses and businesses. Technologically spiffy, even by today's standards.

The Plato terminals were loaded with thousands of computer-aided learning courses. But the main thing that students wanted to do was play games. Were it not for the watchful eyes of human monitors, every expensive terminal would have been running Airwar or Orbit-Blaster.

Two decades later, I still remember how to program those

Plato machines—utterly obsolete knowledge—but I've completely forgotten the dozen on-line courses I took. All that educational content, developed at great expense, simply never stuck.

Public school administrators often promote distance education as a cure for the one-room rural schoolhouse . . . it's a way for the kid out on the farm to take classes which aren't normally offered out in the sticks. The educational cliché is that distance education helps level the playing field.*

Sounds fine—any rural student can take an electronic course in post-modern literary analysis. But I'll bet they won't, just as city kids aren't going to sign up for distance education classes in animal husbandry.

The distance learner receives a sterilized version of a course which hasn't the impact or fascination of the live course. Five field trips to a forest will teach far more about ecology than a hundred Web sites; a week of instruction on a lathe will create a more skilled mechanic than a year of down-linked satellite video.

Stripped of its electronic glitz, distance education is a whisper away from the 1930s' correspondence schools. "Learn in your own home," "Get a good education and step up to higher pay!," "In the comfort of your living room, ten famous writers will teach you the easy way to a literary fortune." All this from home-study courses brought by mail.

At the turn of the century, the Victrola was seen as a

---

* In at least one Texas school, the distance education center is heavily used mainly because it's the only classroom with air conditioning.

revolutionary method that would allow anyone to easily learn a foreign language. I remember my mom studiously listening to French while stewing tomatoes on the stove top. Years of home study never got her much past "parlez-vous français?" but she kept plugging, a true believer in home study and the power of technological teaching. Hey—tourists still purchase cassettes in hopes of becoming fluent in French on the plane to Paris. Does anyone ever learn much from 'em?

Why did learn-by-mail fail? Correspondence schools' dropout rates often exceeded 50 percent. In some cases, correspondence schools counted on only a few incoming students completing the course of study. Naturally, the promoters demanded most of the fees up front . . . dropouts paid almost as much as graduates. Their profits came from the dropouts.

Hucksters of the electronic classroom will show you studies that prove on-line learning outcomes equal if not better face-to-face instruction. Uh, right.

At Vanderbilt University, the Asynchronous Learning Network gives a series of technology workshops over the Internet. Moderators post assignments and facilitators assist with the usual technical problems—"My password won't work," "I can't get to this file" . . . You know the stuff.

Well, each student fronted $250 for an eight-week workshop on how to build an on-line course. These are students from around the world—faculty from community colleges, government officials, librarians, professionals, even a few homemakers. An ideal application of interactive technology, right?

Despite the best intentions of educational technologists, the program flopped. Of course, the promoters won't say so—they're still offering the course. But flop it did. Two hundred fifty students registered and began dropping out at an exponential rate: Four weeks into the course, only a quarter still participated. Only three finished the required course work. Exactly one student completed all the work.

How come? Well, technical problems showed up: It took a long time to log on, many students didn't understand how to navigate the material, those with slow modems were frustrated.

Then, too, each student was daily confronted with dozens, if not hundreds, of messages—many utterly trivial, some inane, some useful, and others simply irrelevant. Students complained that they simply didn't have the time to process all this information. The beginners were overwhelmed; experts were bored. Both dropped out.

But deeper problems showed up. The electronic classroom lacks any sense of community. Students never met each other. They never met their teachers. Naturally, they developed zero commitment to the class.

Those facilitators—and there were plenty of 'em—gave technical support. But they didn't help students with the course work, nor could they provide even the minimal level of encouragement that a lowly TA would in a real class.

The instructors hoped that students would help each other out . . . students aiding students. Naturally, peer-to-peer teaching fails—students make lousy teachers. Nobody registers for a class and expects another student to teach. You want an expert—a professor. But in this on-line workshop, there wasn't a prof. Just a bunch of facilitators.

These workshops were funded by the Sloan Foundation. Naturally, the Vanderbilt workshops were advertised as a success. Because of the "success" of this workshop, the Sloan Foundation renewed Vanderbilt's grant for their one-stop shop for on-line learning resources. Other educational granting agencies such as Annenberg/CPB and the National Science Foundation strongly fund distance learning and related "innovative learning technologies."

No pilot project in educational technology has ever been declared a failure. Perhaps there's an underground of skeptics among the techno-educators, but most have been cloyed by a river of money flowing into such "research" projects. Who do you think gets grants: those who promise wonders from electronic classrooms or those who challenge their results?

Sixteen states cooperated to form the Western Governors University, a computer-based distance learning system. With a staff of twenty and a budget of $9.5 million, this virtual university doesn't offer its own classes, but serves as a broker for Internet and video classes taught by other colleges. They had sold the project to the states, claiming that some five thousand students would sign up in the first year for traditional distance education courses.

In September 1998, some one thousand students inquired about classes. Within a month, the total enrollment was exactly ten.

"It would have been great to have a massive enrollment

when we first opened," said Jeff Edwards, WGU's director of marketing. "We're finding students want to know more. They want to find out about the university, how it works." Trying to place this fiasco in the best light, another marketing spokesman reported that the school was processing seventy-five more applications.

Ten million dollars and fewer than a hundred students. They'd be money ahead if they paid each student fifty grand to attend a real university.

Today's pressure for distance education grows in part from the commercialization of higher education. Research, once considered a high academic calling, is now a profit center for major universities. In turn, education itself is a product, as courses are sold on CD-ROMs, Web sites, and videotapes. No surprise to hear of copyrighting of lectures and legal battles over the ownership of electronic rights to class lectures.

College administrators, watching the growth of their campus electronic networks, have naturally assumed that there's a real demand for distance education. Clichés like "the virtual campus" and "lifelong learning" created inflated expectations for the profitability of distance learning. So over the past few years, most universities have installed elaborate multimedia studios and satellite uplinks.

But slowly, it's becoming obvious that there just isn't a big market for distance education. Those with jobs apparently aren't yearning for college course work. And surprisingly few individuals, whether homebound or at work, are willing to pay for instruction via the tube.

Having committed serious funds to these projects, college administrators now wonder what to do with their electronic marvels. Increasingly, they're turning inward: replacing live classrooms with pre-taped seminars.

Rather than pay a professor to teach a course on campus, colleges simply show a videotaped lecture from some famous speaker. This cuts down on classroom space by bringing lectures into dormitories, lets students "attend" class at any hour, and allows foreign students to study via the Internet. And, in a circular reasoning, it justifies the expenditure in wiring the buildings.

Such "e-courses" and "video tutorials" substitute videotapes and Web pages for expensive professors. The college can service more students with fewer staff. And it's a captive market—when freshman chemistry is taught on the tube, students don't have any choice in the matter. The result is a digital diploma mill, where students pay tuition to watch instructional television.

Suppose the electronic classroom actually succeeds. I'll bet the second-tier schools will wind up with electronic courses and video instruction. Their instructors will hand out assignments over the Web and chiefly interact with students via e-mail. Desiccated course work will be spiced up with video clips and occasional games. Rows of wooden desks will be replaced by rooms of sterile computer monitors. Who'll get the live teachers? The affluent, of course.

Distance learning? It's an excellent way to get a third-rate education.

Cyberschool

Welcome to the classroom of the future! Complete with electronic links to the world, it'll revolutionize education. Students will interact with information infrastructures and knowledge processors to learn group work and telework, whatever that means. You'll be enriched, empowered, and enabled by the digital classroom; immersed in an optimal learning environment. Yee-ha!

Worried that things rarely turn out as promised? Well, let me present a pessimal* view of the schoolroom of the future.

Suppose you're a harried school board member. Voters complain about high taxes. Teachers' unions strike for higher wages and smaller classes. Parents worry about plummeting scores on standardized tests. Newspapers criticize backward teaching methods, outdated textbooks, and security problems.

---

* The opposite of optimal?

Unruly students cut classes and rarely pay attention. Instructors teach topics which aren't in the curriculum or, worse, inject their own opinions into subject matter.

Sound like a tough call? Naw—it's easy to solve all these problems, placate the taxpayers, and get re-elected. High technology!

First, the school district buys a computer for every student. Sure, this'll set back the budget—maybe a few hundred dollars per student. Quantity discounts and corporate support should keep the price down, and classroom savings will more than offset the cost of the equipment.

Next buy a pile of CD-ROMs for the students, each pre-programmed with fun edutainment programs. The educational games will exactly cover the curriculum . . . for every paragraph in the syllabus, the game will have an interactive aspect. As students climb to more advanced levels, the game naturally becomes more challenging and rewarding. But always fun.

Every student will work at her own pace. The youngest will watch happy cartoon characters and exciting animations. The kid that likes horses will listen to messages from a chatty pony; the child that dreams of fire engines will hear from Fred the Firefighter. High schoolers get multimedia images of film stars and rock and roll celebrities. With access to interactive video sessions, chat rooms, and e-mail, students can collaborate with each other. It's the ultimate in individualized, child-centered instruction.

Naturally, the edu-games will be programmed so that students become adept at standardized tests. No reason to teach anything that's not on the ACT, PSAT, or SAT exams. And the students will have fun because all this information will be built into games like Myst, Dungeon, or Doom. They'll master the games, and automatically learn the material.

Meanwhile, the computers will keep score, like pinball machines. They'll send e-mail to parents and administrators . . . scores that will become part of each kid's permanent record. No more subjectivity in grading: The principal will know instantly how each child's doing. And if a student gets confused or falls behind, automated help will be just a mouse click away.

We'll update crowded classrooms, too. Replace desks with individual cubicles, comfortable chairs, and multimedia monitors. With no outside interruptions, kids' attention will be directed into the approved creative learning experiences, built into the software. Well compartmentalized, students will hardly ever see other . . . neatly ending classroom discipline problems.

Naturally, teachers are an unnecessary appendix at this cyberschool. No need for 'em when there's a fun, multimedia system at each student's fingertips. Should a student have a question, they can turn to the latest on-line encyclopedia, enter an electronic chat room, or send e-mail to a professional educator. Those laid-off teachers can be retrained as data entry clerks.

As librarians and teachers become irrelevant, they'll be replaced by a cadre of instructional specialists, consultants, and professional hall monitors. Any discipline problems could be handled by trained security guards, who'd monitor the cubicles via remote video links.

Effect? With no more wasted time on student-teacher interactions or off-topic discussions, education will become more efficient. Since the computers' content would be directed at maximizing test performance, standardized test scores will zoom.

Eliminating teachers and luxuries such as art lessons and field trips will save enough to recoup the cost of those fancy computers. With a little effort, this electronic education could even become a profit center. Merely sell advertising space in the edutainment programs. Corporate sponsors, eager to market their messages to impressionable minds, would pay school systems to plug their products within the coursework.

Concerned that such a system might be dehumanizing? Not to worry. Interactive chat sessions will encourage a sense of community and enhance kids' social skills. Should a student have questions, the Internet will put her in instant touch with a trained support mentor. When necessary, real-time instructors will appear on the distance learning displays, available to interact via two-way video.

The Cyberschool will showcase technology and train students for the upcoming electronic workplace. As local employment prospects change, the school board will issue updates to the curriculum over its interactive Web site. And the school board will monitor what each student learns—without idiosyncratic teachers to raise unpopular topics or challenge accepted beliefs.

Advanced students can sign up for on-line extracurricular activities—perhaps joining the Virtual Compassion Corps.

There, students will be paired up across racial, gender, and class lines. Our children would offer foreigners advice and even arrange interviews with prospective employers. In this way, students will perform community service and mentor others, while displaying their cultural awareness over the network. All without ever having to shake hands with a real person, travel to a distant country, or (gasp!) face the real problems of another culture.* Simple, safe, and sterile.

Should parents worry about Johnny's progress, they need only log in over the Internet to see their son's latest test scores. In addition, they'll receive e-mailed reports summarizing their child's work. And at any time, they can click on an icon to see live images of their young scholar, automatically uploaded by a school video camera.

Yep, just sign up for the future: the parent-pleasin', tax-savin', teacher-firin', interactive-educatin', child-centerin' Cyberschool. No stuffy classrooms. No more teacher strikes. No outdated textbooks. No expensive clarinet lessons. No boring homework. No learning. Coming soon to a school district near you.†

---

* An actual proposal from the director of MIT's Laboratory for Computer Science, Michael Dertouzos.

† Idea for a computer game: Cyberschool Superintendent. Players score by saving money. They could eliminate teachers, close libraries, or blow up music studios. Competitors advance by wiring schools, adding computers, and plugging in multimedia systems. Evil monsters might appear in the form of teachers, scholars, and librarians who insist that you read a book. Bonus points, labeled Pilot Project Grants, would be awarded for writing vapid press releases.

2.

The Computer Contrarian

Arrogance of the Techies

I've invested my life in science and technology. But I'm a skeptic. My questioning grows not from a distaste of computing, but rather because I love computers. I worry that the field is mired in hyperbole and overpromotion. These absurd predictions create inflated expectations and ultimately, the loss of credibility.

While technologists happily predict the future, they seem inordinately sensitive to criticism. Should you write an editorial confronting the government, nobody calls you an anarchist. Publish a book that's critical of the Pope and even a devout Catholic won't accuse you of being an atheist. But exert a healthy skepticism toward computers, and you're labeled "Luddite" and told to live in a cave without electricity or water.*

Contrast the geologists who predicted oil shortages with the

---

* Not exactly the same as spelunking. Most caves I've explored have had water. And mud.

nuclear power promoters who promised free electricity. In 1935, the American Association of Petroleum Geologists reported that our nation's oil reserves were quickly being depleted. "Within the next ten years, America will no longer have an oil surplus, and will have to begin importing oil." They went on to say that such imports would have profound effects not only on industry, but also on foreign policy. Not bad . . . the geologists foresaw oil shortages and the rise of OPEC.

Five years later, Robert Hutchens, chancellor of the University of Chicago, predicted that nuclear energy would be the greatest invention since the discovery of fire, transforming American society as dramatically as electrification. In 1954, the chairman of the Atomic Energy Commission predicted that by 1969, electrical energy would be too cheap to meter. Technologists, using pie-in-the-sky prognostication, pointed our nation's energy policy toward nuclear energy and evaded any real public debate.

In the wake of these predictions, look what's happened to the credibility of petroleum geologists and nuclear engineers. The geologists (though not the oil companies) are held in high public regard; nuclear engineers are in such low repute that the profession is the regular butt of jokes on *The Simpsons* cartoon series.

In a similar way, computer professionals don't speak out against the hyperbole and exaggerated promises of the techno-hucksters. Lacking skeptical and critical voices, the field's credibility is eroded, with long-term results of distrust and cynicism.

For quality engineering makes small promises and delivers

big. Yet across the spectrum of computing, I hear predictions bordering on fantasy, with surprisingly little delivered.

In *The Technological Bluff,* Jacques Ellul writes, "When technocrats talk about democracy, ecology, culture, the Third World, or politics, they are touchingly simplistic and annoyingly arrogant."

You bet. Futurists view computing as a pathway to Tomorrowland, where the Internet will somehow bring freedom, diversity, and well-being.

Listen to George Gilder describe changes from 1994 to 2004: "Over the next decade, computer networks will expand their bandwidth by factors of thousands and reconstruct the entire U.S. economy in their image. TV will expire and transpire into a new cornucopia of choice and empowerment . . . video culture will transcend its current mass-media doldrums . . . Hollywood and Wall Street will totter and diffuse to all points of the nation and the globe . . . The most deprived ghetto child in the most blighted project will gain educational opportunities exceeding those of today's suburban preppie."

TV will expire and become a cornucopia of empowerment? Hollywood and Wall Street totter? Ghetto kids will gain vast educational opportunities? Yep . . . just around the corner, an electronic Shangri-La.

John Perry Barlow says that the Internet is the greatest invention since the discovery of fire. He looks to a future where there are no jobs, where technology makes workers "reconfigurable" free agents, and where barter is the universal means of trade. On the Third World, well, "All it would take for Africa to leapfrog into the wonderland of an information economy would be to attach the electrodes."

Worried about unemployment or economic exploitation? No problem . . . just log on! Reminds me of General Electric's 1960s hyperbole: "Progress is our most important product."

Kevin Kelly, editor of *Wired* magazine, sees information displacing materials: "Take away the mass of radiator, axle, and drive shaft by substituting networked chips . . . Once we see cars as chips with wheels, it's easier to imagine airplanes as chips with wings, farms as chips with soil, houses as chips with inhabitants. Yes, they will have mass, but that mass will be subjugated by the overwhelming amount of knowledge and information flowing through it . . . as if they had no mass at all."

Farms, houses, cars don't matter. Just information. We'll solve the housing crunch by building virtual homes complete with hot and cold running data. When our children grow up, they'll want the information and knowledge of a sports car . . . not a physical thing with a radiator and driveshaft. Uh, sure.

Here's Nicholas Negroponte of the MIT Media Lab: "While the politicians struggle with the baggage of history, a new generation is emerging from the digital landscape free of many of the old prejudices. These kids are released from the limitation of geographic proximity as the sole basis of friendship, collaboration, play, and neighborhood. Digital technology can be a natural force drawing people into greater world harmony."

Aah, world harmony through technology! A pathway

which obliterates geography, history, and prejudice. A digital panacea for mankind's blights.

Co-founder of Lotus Corporation Mitch Kapor puts it this way: "Life in cyberspace seems to be shaping up exactly like Thomas Jefferson would have wanted: founded on primacy of individual liberty and a commitment to pluralism, diversity, and community." A democracy populated mostly by white males, dominated by economically well-off North Americans, where Third World citizens mainly speak English, one might add.

These utopian ideals infect politicians. In 1993, Al Gore said, "In the next decade it will be possible for an elementary school student to come home after class and instead of playing Nintendo, plug into the Library of Congress and explore an entire universe of information."

Yep, kids of 2003 will be able to see the catalog of the Library of Congress. But they won't want to. They'll still play Nintendo, watch TV, and when they're on-line, visit the MTV home page. They sure won't be clustered around their terminals merrily plugged into the Library of Congress.

Much of the blather about future electronic worlds is essentially conservative: The self-anointed digerati yearn for classical ideals of community, democracy, and connection. Without any discomfort, they see the Internet simultaneously providing unity and diversity, privacy and community, entertainment and education.

Many of these futurists point to an exponential growth of technology in our time. However, mankind's technological developments have always grown at an exponential rate. And such curves always appear to sweep toward the sky.

Nor are today's inventions more important or more socially shattering than those of a century ago. For example, consider the many pioneering inventions of the late nineteenth century: the telephone, the phonograph, movies, radio, and the internal combustion engine. Hard to think of five such inventions of the late twentieth century. Is the Internet more revolutionary than the telephone? Does the Web affect more people than the car?

The utopian promotion of technology has a long history. In the 1860s, poets wrote elegies about how the transatlantic cable would end war—after all, instant communication will prevent misunderstandings. Newspaper editorials of 1890 praised the telephone as tool of democracy, allowing citizens to bypass the palace guard and directly call the president.

Contrast today's dazzled reaction to instant worldwide communications with the similar amazement of a century ago. For instance, in 1874, one David Perkins of Manchester wrote to a friend on his eighty-sixth birthday:

> One of our neighbors, a widow lady, recently expressed the wish to live five hundred years longer. I said in reply that during her short life she had seen greater advancement in the arts and sciences, greater improvements, adapted to make men wiser and better, than had ever before occurred during any five hundred years of the world's history.
>
> Look over your life today, my friend, and consider how eventful it has been, and how much you have accomplished

for good. What rapid studies have been made in all the elements of greatness.

Your eighty-six years have revolutionized the world. Men everywhere occupy a higher plane today than when your eyes first beheld the light. Distance has been annihilated—all nature has been brought with subjection to your will—you send your thoughts to your friends by the lightning and use the sun in heaven to paint their portraits.

In view of the great things you have seen in your day and generation, how thankful you are and how thankful we all should be to our Heavenly Father for giving us life and living in this age . . .

Somehow, I doubt that the octogenarian recipient shared such wonderment for the photograph, railroad, and telegraph. And though it's been a century since we annihilated distance, kids are still being taught the cliché of a shrinking globe. If nineteenth-century inventions subjugated nature to our will, what is the legacy of the twentieth? Today, are we living on a higher plane thanks to the Internet, cell phones, and high-definition television?

In the 1930s rural electrification was supposed to save the family farm. After three decades of extensive promotion and wire stringing, all the farms were wired. So where's that family farm today? Gone.

In the 1950s, television was promoted as a boon for education. It would bring the finest educators into the classrooms and homes of even the poorest families. That genuinely happened, thanks to governmental subsidies to broadcast stations and extensive grants for educational programming. What happened to the great educational boon that was supposed to follow?

Promoters in the early 1980s glibly stated that communications satellites would encourage global unity through worldwide television. Unity through MTV, perhaps.

Today's futurists continue to tell us that the world is shrinking, thanks to travel, communications, and commerce. As evidence of the ever smaller globe, they'll point to McDonald's in Paris, Moscow, and Beijing. Nairobi teenagers' T-shirts now sport Coca-Cola logos. But we're no closer to any foreign culture.

What's really shrinking is the American view of the world: We are unable to speak foreign languages, unwilling to read foreign news, and unequipped to understand foreign cultures. We naturally perceive other cultures the easy way: by watching them on TV or glimpsing them through a porthole of the Internet. This conveys images, not understanding. Rather than shrinking our globe, this shallow electronic information system makes foreign cultures more distant.

Technologists want us to believe that they've got the future in a hammerlock, speaking glowingly of intelligent search agents, virtual reality shopping, and computer-mediated education. Journalists believe 'em, too—when reporters write about life in the coming decades, they tend to seek out computer entrepreneurs.

But engineers are hardly noted for breadth of vision. Computer jocks make excellent programmers. Some are great at selling software and making money. But programming and promotion have nothing to do with prognostication. Bill Gates may be an excellent businessman and software designer. But, like Henry Ford and Thomas Edison, he sees the future in terms of the technology that he's comfortable with.

Computer experts waste enormous resources by making grandiose predictions. An obsession with expert systems and artificial intelligence sucked billions of dollars into fabled "Fifth Generation" systems. Virtual Reality Markup Language was going to show the Web in full three dimensions. Push technology would magically download the information we needed before we even asked for it. Investors rushed to fund network portals, which would direct our attention to the best network avenues. Network computers would work without disks by hooking up directly over the Internet. Electronic commerce, based on cryptographic payment systems, would bring a whole new model for doing business. Intelligent agents would filter our mail, pick our movies, and tell us where to shop. Our lives would be revolutionized by social interfaces, interactive television, and resource visualization. All came to naught.

Journalists go along uncritically; when the media coverage disappears, the fads evaporate and companies slide into oblivion. For example, Digicash, Inc. promised mathematically secure cash transfers across the net with almost no transfer fees. Luminary Nicholas Negroponte called it "The most exciting product I have seen in the past twenty years." Following the heavy coverage in newspapers, investors flocked to the company, believing that software would make paper money obsolete. Five years and millions of dollars later, Digicash went bankrupt. Few reporters had noticed that old-fashioned credit cards were quite adequate for making electronic payments.

As fads sweep across technology, schools go along for the ride. John M. Broughton of Columbia Teachers College notes that "The tradition of grossly inflated claims identified in the artificial intelligence literature . . . appears to have carried over into the area of electronic learning."

When I wonder about the future, I listen to historians. Sociologists. Psychologists. Want to know what people will be like in ten or twenty years? Ask a schoolteacher.

I'm a licensed propeller head: astronomer, computer jock, and Internet user. Were I just a kindergarten teacher who didn't sit behind a monitor, technocrats would arrogantly push me aside, saying, "You aren't on-line, so you don't know of the great benefits of the Internet, and you have no right to criticize it." It's a little like saying, "Hey, if you're not a nuclear power engineer, then you don't understand atomic energy enough to criticize it. Trust us. We're experts."

Well, I don't trust experts. I don't trust futurists. Although I'm reputed to be a computer expert, nobody ever gave me a crystal ball.

Still, I can make a few guesses about life in a hundred years. Forget predictions of gyrocopters, magnetic-levitated monorails, cheap nuclear power, robotic surgeons, and electronic brain connections. Most likely, we'll have pretty much the same problems of today, magnified by a greater population, fewer resources, and less face-to-face interaction.

Hey—come hop in my time machine. As a physicist, I can do that . . . after all, we own space and time. You might recall Professor Peabody's Way Back machine—the gizmo that would propel cartoon characters back into history. Well, just pop the batteries in backward, and you'll wind up in the future.

So just spin the dials to the year 2100, press that red button, and—ping—you're here at the dawn of the twenty-second century. First thing you'll notice is that we're all dead. Almost everyone from the twentieth century is dead. Most of our *children* are dead. Our grandkids now run the country, and our great-grandchildren complain about it.

What jobs will be around in 2100? Surprise! They're pretty much the same jobs available today: dentists, truck drivers, surgeons, ballet dancers, salespeople, entertainers, and school-teachers. A century from now, there will still be movie stars, morticians, gardeners, forest rangers, and police officers, Yep, in a hundred years, we'll still have lawyers and politicians, though we might wish otherwise.

Curious thing about all those jobs—none of them require computing. The main skill of a dentist is the ability to fix and maintain teeth, and to do so with as little discomfort as possible. That's a skill that you can't download from any Web site. Who'd visit a dentist whose experience in root canals came from a multimedia CD-ROM?

There's another skill that every good dentist needs—

whether in 2000 or 2100. The ability to inspire confidence and trust. It might show up as a pat on the shoulder. "After the Novocain wears off, your tooth may hurt," she'll say. "But in a week, your tooth will feel fine. Trust me."

Trust. The ability to inspire confidence. Today, you can't get that from the Internet. A hundred years from now, the ability to deal with people still won't be learned from a computer. Quite the opposite: The hours spent prowling across the Internet are hours that dull the very skills necessary to get along with others. If we wish to create a world of isolates—a society where people cannot get along with each other—I can hardly think of a better way than to shove children into cyberspace and tell 'em to communicate electronically.

Today, I've rarely heard of anyone dismissed for inadequate computer skills. People mainly get fired for being unable to get along with others. Tomorrow's jobs, like today's, will belong to those with social skills. Yet the time we spend behind a keyboard dulls those essential abilities.

In the world of 2100, I'll bet that we'll still need plumbers . . . somehow, I can't imagine drainpipes will be unclogged by clicking on an Internet icon. Where will those twenty-second-century plumbers learn their craft?

Today in the San Francisco Bay Area, Web programmers get forty or fifty dollars an hour . . . pretty good wages. Yet plumbers charge more than twice as much. How come?

Part of the reason for that expense is overhead—a plumber needs a truckload of tools, while the programmer's content with a computer and phone line. A part of the disparity is due to immediacy: I can live quite well for a month without a computer. But when my kitchen sink's plugged up, I need a plumber right away.

But there's another, overlooked reason for the price difference between plumbers and programmers. Around San Francisco, almost every school teaches computing. Almost none teach the trades: auto mechanics, cabinet making, or plumbing. Which do we need more: another programmer or a competent mechanic?

Today, we're pushing most everyone into computing. But I don't care if my plumber keeps a fancy Web page. I want him to know how pipes work. When every student—good and bad—is pressed to become a computer maven, and only the incompetents are allowed to become plumbers, neither our programs nor our pipes will hold water.

As computing siphons off brilliant people, what's happening to our artists? One reason for the great art of Renaissance Florence was patron support for the creative. Today's creative talent is funneled into television, computing, and Web page design. They're paid to express commercial messages with animation.

Other important skills in life can't be learned from the Internet. The ability to stand up and speak to an audience. Dexterity with a musical instrument. The confidence to make a cold sales call. The gift of party banter. The ability to catch a fly ball—several baseball scouts blame America's scarcity of pitchers on kids' love affair with computer games.

This obsession with a digital world affects political decisions. Communities clamor for high-tech jobs, giving tax breaks to such businesses and funding technology promotions. So we hear of British Columbia developing a Silicon Forest. Mendocino County in California will become the Silicon Coast. There's a Silicon Prairie in Kansas, a Silicon Glen in Scotland. Probably Egypt has a Silicon Wadi. These endeavors attempt to nurture high-tech industrial development through government subsidies.

As a result, we find British Columbia spending a hundred million dollars to create the BC Institute of Technology. They're creating a campus with close links to high-tech industry. "*What* high-tech industry in western Canada?" you may ask. Oh, it'll arrive once we build the university, they'll argue back. But the university depends on those links for teaching, so, uh . . .

If computers form our culture's manifest destiny, they shouldn't *need* public funding . . . they'll grow and thrive without governmental support. At the same time that states form incubators for high-tech jobs, computer industry leaders tell us of shortages in high-tech industries—Canada needs fifty thousand more computer programmers, the United States must invite a hundred thousand foreign workers to fill the gap. What's wrong with this picture?

In the future, what'll happen to the digerati? As the Internet becomes accepted into our culture, I'll bet that they'll no longer form the ramparts of the future. If anything, having become so vested in the Internet, they'll be the defenders of an electronic status quo. I won't be surprised if they turn to government to preserve the virtual communities which today seem so avant-garde and countercultural.

Me? I'll probably remain a skeptic. Distance may have been annihilated and lightning may send my thoughts, but there are still plenty of inflated claims waiting to be deflated.

Tired of looking around the future? Jump back in my time machine and I'll spin the dial to a time when we're wiser and so much more hip. Whoops—that's 1969. I'll get it right one of these days.

Software Guinea Pigs

Software testing. It's expensive. Unpredictable. Time-consuming. And it's slowly disappearing.

Yep, in these days of buggy software, when minor improvements are touted as revolutionary, companies seem loath to test software.

Can't blame 'em: Features sell software, not testing. Hard to imagine a program being promoted as "well tested" or "reliable."

Yet there's no other way to guarantee good programs. Software makers have long promised tools to generate perfect programs—hey, the first compilers were created to make error-free code. Computer scientists search for formal proofs of logical consistency.

But software tools can't generate good code from bad assumptions. And formal logic systems won't check that two programs work alongside each other. Sadly, testing remains the only way to confidently eliminate bugs.

Testing software costs money. Software companies must try their products on different machines, with both old and new hardware. They probably rely on both in-house testers and competent volunteers, which means coordinating efforts and checking that all parts of the system get tested.

Volunteers? Well, not exactly. Plenty of users step forward to receive copies to test, but most don't submit new problems. Testing software requires patience, a dogged diligence to explore every possible combination of entries, and a willingness to actually document all the blind alleys explored . . . qualities not freely available among volunteers. And so, programming companies employ software testers who slave—rarely recognized and never thanked—for the lowest salaries in the company. Why pay big bucks for someone to find your mistakes?

Testing chews up time just when the program's overdue and almost out the door. The closer the company comes to shipping, the more complex the tests. Testing people slow things down at the very moment that marketing folks want to show off their new baby.

Nobody agrees on what constitutes a well-tested program or when it's adequately debugged. There's alpha testing, where the software stays in-house. Beta testing goes out to field testers, recruited from avid fans and professional computer jocks. At the end of the rainbow lies the golden release—a bug-free, commercially successful program that's reliable, robust, and long-lived.

At least that's the dream. With widespread Internet connections, beta-test software is increasingly sold on-line as "early release" software. Then, as software writers receive and digest bug reports and complaints, new revisions get posted to the net. So programs just don't get tested much . . . perhaps less than in the past. Bugs that result in crashes—showstoppers—may go undetected due to poor testing. Program developers, already antsy to get on with another project, may simply downgrade or ignore bug reports.

About the only people who appreciate software testing are the end users. As today's software companies release half-baked programs, it's we who pay to test their software: whenever a crash chews up our time behind the screen. And we pay again when we purchase an upgrade to eradicate that bug. A problem in my disk repair software destroyed a week of my work. I looked to the Web and found this solution: Buy an updated copy of the same program.

It's as if those ballyhooed Total Quality Management programs apply to manufacturers, but not software developers. Zero defects seems to be a wonderful goal for transmission assembly lines, but not programs.

We've become accepting of buggy software. In 1996, when an Intel microprocessor was sold with an obscure arithmetic error, many attacked the chipmaker. But operating systems regularly crash and software is often internally incompatible, yet we tolerate it, trusting that it'll be patched in the next release.

Is every program a work in progress . . . never to be complete, never to be bug-free? If so, computing will forever be expensive, since we'll constantly have to support leagues of programmers, continually repairing their own creations. If only there were a magic way to make quality programs which didn't need to be maintained.

Alas, in computing, as in education and urban renewal, there's no magic. Almost anyone can write a program, but it takes foresight, discipline, and perseverance to build a successful programming product.

It's impossible to discuss compilers and computer bugs without a nod to Grace Murray Hopper. In the 1940s, the Navy assigned Ensign Hopper to work on the Mark I computer at Harvard's Computation Laboratory. Using that early machine to create trigonometric tables, she was one of the first programmers.*

Grace Hopper would create the first computer language, Flow-matic, which mapped English words into computer commands. Her work evolved into Cobol, for a quarter century the language of choice for business computing. At least as impor-

---

* She's said to have invented the word "bug" to describe a defect in a machine, after finding a moth squashed in the contacts of a computer's relay. But the etymology (and entomology) of the word goes back to another inventor. In 1889, the *Pall Mall Gazette* reported, "Mr. Edison had been up the two previous nights discovering 'a bug' in his phonograph—an expression for solving a difficulty, and implying that some imaginary insect has secreted itself inside and is causing all the trouble."

tant, she invented the idea of a subroutine—separate code frag-ments which could be linked together to make a complete program.

Like many other computing pioneers, Grace Hopper saw a revolutionary role for technology. "It is the current aim," she said in 1952, "to replace, as far as possible, the human brain by an electronic digital computer." Thanks a bunch, most of us would reply.

Years after developing the foundations of modern com-puting, Grace Hopper—by then Rear Admiral Hopper—real-ized that computing, rather than saving money for the government, was swallowing enormous amounts of cash. Over half the cost of NASA's space shuttle, for example, would pour into developing and maintaining software. Grace Hopper hoped that standards would help solve the problem: Common languages would be the path to quality program-ming.

Alas, just as standardizing English doesn't eliminate misun-derstandings and arguments, standardized computer languages haven't eliminated bugs and crashes. You can write buggy pro-grams in any computer language. Programming errors were once mainly the result of typos or failing to align columns when keypunching. Today, they're more likely due to misun-derstanding an interface between operating system and pro-gram, or perhaps the failure to check the bounds on incoming data.

Oh, if only a universal computer language could solve pro-gramming errors! Consider some of the languages of the past, each staking a claim as the standard of the future: Cobol, Fortran, ADA, Snobol, PL1 Lisp, Focal, APL, Forth, Bliss, Basic, C, C++, HTML, Perl, VRML, Java . . . I've coded in each of these dialects and every few years another appears. Each gave me a new way to express myself; each provided new ways to make mistakes. And none of them relieved me of the need to test my software.

Worse, a menagerie of disk drives, monitors, and memory configurations conspire against the universal program. Some small systems haven't been upgraded since 1986, others run the latest undocumented Microsoft system upgrades. Much as you want to write clean, sophisticated code, you still have to support warty old platforms like DOS.

Probably the biggest headache in testing is interaction between programs. As long as you're testing an isolated program on one computer, you stand a chance of exploring most of the trouble spots. But with a half-dozen different operating systems and hundreds of possible programs running alongside yours, well, there's no comprehensive test suite. It's tough just to get repeatable crashes.

Most computer problems show up at two times: when the system's new and when it's old. The first bugs come from the new system—installation problems, incompatible software, training frustrations. New features conflict with established programs. Incomplete documentation, inadequately tested applications, badly built software.

As we get past these birthing pains, the system becomes stable—which is to say, we accommodate to its idiosyncrasies.

We put up with the occasional crash and say that the computer works tolerably well.

A few years after installation, problems start popping up more often. The system's too slow. The monitor's too small. The computer can't run the latest upgrade. There's not enough memory to handle certain applications.

Meanwhile, users become more sophisticated and demand more from their computers. Simple word processing isn't enough; we want multiple fonts, graphics, and spell-checkers. Simple e-mail no longer satisfies; we want integrated systems with address books, graphics, and sounds. As we explore more of the application's capabilities, we're bound to stumble over bugs and design shortcomings.

As these defects and limitations cause more and more headaches, eventually it becomes less frustrating to buy a new computer than to tolerate the old system. This drives the software industry on a constant stream of revisions, updates, and upgrades. Yet every improvement creates a new set of problems . . . for every two bugs stomped, a new bug is born. And so, another software cycle begins.

A graph of computing bugs looks like the cross section of a bathtub. Installation blunders and incompatibilities keep aspirin consumption high for the first few weeks. Soon, the system reaches a plateau of productivity—the computer's middle age—followed by a gradual rise in problems.

Sadly, such bathtub curves aren't limited to computers or software. They pop up everywhere. Cars show the most problems during their first months of ownership and last year on

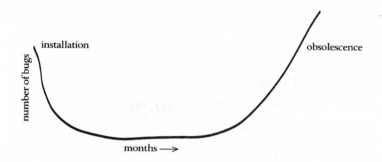

the road. We spend the most on home improvements soon after moving in and just before selling a house. And our most expensive medical problems typically show up during our first months and last years.

Having accepted that owning a computer means a constant upgrade, I realize that today's computers will always seem less than those of tomorrow. The software I've grown accustomed to will sprout new features that I'll have to learn. All the while, I'll be followed by a trail of obsolete technology.

Maybe software testing isn't disappearing. Every time I sit down to my computer, I play the role of software tester. All the while, I dream of the Shangri-La where computers don't crash.

The Tyranny
of the Ugly Computer

hy are computers so *ugly?* Who decided that a million monitors must be pale dove gray? How come I can buy a red shirt, an orange umbrella, a yellow bowling ball, a green radio, and a blue car, but computers are all beige boxes? It's as if Henry Ford ran the computer business: You can have any color you wish, as long as it's off-white putty.

Not exactly—Apple now makes a line of computers with five colors. Alas, except for those color panel inserts, they pretty much look like every other computer.

Think of the many possibilities: An art deco computer case, with the exuberance of the Chrysler building. A monitor shaped like the 1950s Philco Predicta. Or frame the video screen between Corinthian columns, acanthus leaves, and graceful volutes. Maybe a wooden keyboard, made from knotty pine? Anything but sterile box-shaped, post-modern generic gray plastic.

And if you think the toad on your desktop looks ugly, glance at your videotape recorder, microwave oven, stereo, or television. They'd look perfectly at home in an industrial electronics laboratory. Of course, uglification affects more than just technology—look at any strip mall. But it seems that appliance makers have adopted a deliberately nihilistic design aesthetic.

Now look within these unsightly packages. Electronic devices are increasingly afflicted with obnoxious interfaces and annoying assumptions. At least computer designers try (however unsuccessfully) to make their systems easier to operate. Ordinary appliances seem to be built to frustrate.

I'm particularly incensed at the clutter of unnecessary features added to common household fixtures. Phones require programming; easy-to-use cameras demand multiple adjustments; car radios can't be tuned without taking your eyes from the road. Sure, all these come with instruction manuals—but who's going to read a booklet to reprogram their car radio? And within a year, the booklet's gone.

Thanks to microprocessors, simple devices have evolved into a frustrating complexity. Alarm clocks were once pretty simple devices, able to be operated by ordinary citizens. We now deal with digital alarm-radios sprouting fifteen push buttons and three knobs. Does some electronics engineer expect me to program the thing at midnight and deprogram it at 7 A.M.? What do they take me for, a furry-headed Ph.D.?

Those complicated devices aren't just harder to operate.

They're often impossible to maintain. As recently as the 1970s, an AT&T-Bell* technician could come to your house and fix the handset on your telephone. Then, too, those art-deco rotary phones had service lives measured in decades. Think that the white Taiwanese model sitting on your desk will last ten years? Could anyone fix it? Would it be worth fixing?

Gratuitous complexity has quietly crept into what were once called televisions, radios, and stereos. Today, relabeled "modular high-tech home entertainment centers," they sprout scores of cryptically labeled black buttons, camouflaged on black panels and built into black boxes. Graphical equalizers have pushed aside bass-treble knobs; memory banks have replaced tuning dials; programmable function switches take the place of simple controls. Maybe part of the home entertainment is figuring out how to work the thing.

Digital clocks now appear in unlikely and unuseful places . . . I've seen them built into cameras, washing machines, even staplers. I can imagine a doohickey designer saying, "Hey, it doesn't cost much . . ." But it does cost, and not just in ugliness. Those superfluous clocks need attention twice a year with the time changes, not to mention when their batteries inevitably fail. Whatever function they add is paid for in complexity and frustration.

And wristwatches. Whatever happened to watches with big and little hands that you could set by just turning the stem?

The thermostat on my wall was once a brass object which

---

* AT&T stands for American Telephone and Telegraph. I'll bet cookies to doughnuts that they won't supply telegraph service.

was pretty easy to figure out. It switched on the furnace when it was too cold. I'd turn a wheel to adjust the temperature. Today's new homes are legally required to use electronic setback thermostats. Seems like a great idea—reduce the house temperature at night, warm up in the morning and evening. Now, I'm all in favor of conserving energy. But what a messy solution! There are eight buttons and a digital display on my state-of-the-art thermostat. It's thrice as big as the old-style thermostats. Programming the thing took an hour. It needs three batteries, which will someday wear out, forcing me to reprogram the beast. And by then, I'll have forgotten how. Now where is that instruction booklet . . .

Of course, my cutting-edge thermostat assumes that I'll wake up at the same time every day. That I'll return home at the same time. It's a prime example of technological progress making life more difficult.

It reminds me of the long-promised smart house. For decades, architects and electronics buffs have told us of the revolutionary benefits to be gained through electronics. IBM promotes its Home Director System, telling how it will automatically turn on lights when it gets dark and turn them off once you go to bed.

I scoff: Turning on and off the lights just doesn't trouble me. But I bet that programming that Home Director System isn't easy. Like many technological promises, the smart house solves a non-problem while creating a slew of new troubles.

Computer pioneer Bob Frankston lives in an automated house. Still, he asks, "Is your life so predictable that you want your lights turned on at the same time every day?" Naturally, Frankston feels that the electronic house hasn't gone far enough—houses need more automation, including sensors and, yes, Internet links. Within ten years he believes that microwave ovens, dishwashers, and air conditioners will have network jacks. He wants the smart house to become a responsive house.

Predictably, upon recognizing a problem caused by technology, technologists naturally want to layer on still more technology. And so we find Sun Microsystems promoting Jini, a networking system which will allow your cell phone to talk to the furnace, and both to chat with your toaster. You'll be able to set the temperature of your living room from your office cubicle.

Well, I don't want to live in a smart house. Or a responsive house, either. More important to me is that the windows open and the toilet doesn't overflow. I'd rather my house have a fireplace than an Internet-linked dishwasher. As far as making my home responsive, I just wish that the doorbell worked.

Every systems designer should repeat Yale professor David Gelernter's thesis: Technology's most important obligation is to get out of the way. Machinery should make life easier. Useless features and bad design make technology a self-important nuisance instead of a help.

"Information is Power"

I t's the shibboleth of the information age. Power flows to those with fast, ready access to information. The Information Age is an education age, in which education must start at birth and continue throughout a lifetime. After all, the Internet is a technology that empowers.

Bah.

Such tired clichés make me wonder: Just when did the information age begin? Did it begin with the early personal computers in 1980? Was it back in 1964 when Marshall McLuhan first used the term? Were we living in the information age in October 1929, when the stock market crash radioed around the world in minutes? Did 1848 mark the beginning of the information age when Morse sent the first telegram? How about 1733 . . .

I'll bet we've always lived in the information age. But only recently have technocrats arrogantly proclaimed themselves the high priests of a new order. The Internet delivers a mountain of information, but it sure doesn't make anyone powerful.

Information isn't power. Who's got the most information in your neighborhood? Librarians, and they're famous for having no power at all. Who has the most power in your community? Politicians, of course. And they're notorious for being ill informed.

Information isn't money either. I've never met a panhandler on the street corner, hand outstretched, begging for information. Nor have I seen a corporate executive pounding his desk, complaining that the company's profits are going down because they don't produce enough information. Come to think of it, I haven't met anyone yearning for more junk mail. Many problems confront society, but too little information isn't one of them.

Yet Vice President Al Gore worries that unless we invest heavily in the Internet, we will develop into a society of information haves and have-nots. On the surface, this is a red herring: Access to televised information hardly makes better citizens. Should we place TV sets in every classroom? Subsidize newspaper subscriptions for the poor?

There's plenty wrong with our schools—lack of discipline, low interest in scholarship, leaky roofs, politically inspired curricula. But lack of information just isn't a pressing problem. Do the politicians who promote wiring our schools really believe that access to the Internet will bring out a love for mathematics, physics, history, or world affairs?

The equation of information and power is a corruption of Francis Bacon's comment in 1597: "Knowledge is power." Most likely he was referring to Proverbs 24:5: "A wise man is strong; yea, a man of knowledge increaseth strength."

Wisdom and knowledge . . . they're linked to scholarship, ideas, experience, maturity, judgment, perspective, and reflection. But they have little to do with information.* Nor do they have much to do with power.

So how do you get power? Certainly not by accessing lots of information. Were that true, Internet links would endow the digerati with unheard-of strength. Power doesn't grow from knowledge, either. The byways of success are littered with geniuses unable to transform their ideas into reality.

Power—whether in the workplace or the legislature—depends on social skills. Leadership grows from the ability to listen to many sides and make compromises. The strength of character to stay on the right path. The guts to stand up for a just cause.

Social skills. Strength of character. Trust. Determination. Perseverance. Not traits downloadable from a Web site. Quite the opposite: Every hour that you spend with your brain in cyberspace marks sixty minutes you aren't sharpening those

---

* I'm more inclined to agree with Henry Thoreau: "It is said that knowledge is a power . . . What is most of our boasted so-called knowledge but a conceit that we know something, which robs us of the advantages of our actual ignorance."

skills that our world so desperately needs. The best way to create a community of loners is for each of us to escape into the welcoming arms of the Internet.

Remember Faust, that legendary scholar who sold his soul to the devil? Dr. Faust was a real person, though his sixteenth-century colleagues considered him a fraud and humbug. He boasted that if all the works of Aristotle and Plato were blotted from the memory of man, he could restore them with greater elegance. And Faust shrugged at Christ's miracles; after all, he could do the same whenever he wished. Having spread the rumor that he was in league with the devil, it's hardly surprising that Magister Georgius Sabellicus Faustus J. was chased out of towns and apparently carried off in 1525.

With poetic license and no little embroidery, Goethe wrote of Faust living a tired scholar's esoteric existence. Seeking deeper knowledge and greater powers, he summons up the spirits: "I am Faust, in every way your equal." He traps Mephistopheles with a pentagram, demanding knowledge and power. Mephistopheles snickers: "Knowledge and power, eh? That can be arranged . . ."

Oh, but Faust had a price to pay. Call him Mr. Scratch, the prince of darkness, Beelzebub, or Mephistopheles, the devil demands his due: Faust's immortal soul.

Jump forward to the beginning of the twenty-first century. Scholars everywhere summon up the Internet: Just sign up, log on, and open your mind to a universe of information and power. Omniscience and omnipotence, right at your fingertips.

Price? Just listen to the Internet promoters: All this information is free! But on-line, we surrender something far more valuable than dollars. Mephisto of the modem demands a most precious resource—our time on earth.

We're accustomed to the passage of time in work, school, sports, and even television. Meetings and meals break up the workday. Intermissions and end-games tell us a game's progress. Classes wind up after fifty minutes. Commercials remind us of the passage of television time.

But the computer monitor shows no such milestones. On-line, time slips by neither milestone nor reminder. Hours flow out my modem, as my mind follows links and cross-references. I'm awash in information, with control of my cybernetic destiny. Knowledge and power!

Yet am I more powerful when I sign off? Do I know more than if I'd spent the time reading a book? Am in closer touch with my friends and family?

I can imagine Faust's Mephisto rubbing his hands in glee.

But this isn't just a single pact with yonder devil. Schools, organizations, whole governments encourage us to log on. Across the world, we're pressed to surrender our physical surroundings for the virtual. What'll be the social effect of millions of people connected to the Internet?

Sociologist Robert D. Putnam researched how American communities have changed over the past fifty years. He refers to "social capital"—the features of society such as norms, trust, and interaction that promote cooperation for mutual benefit. His paper "Bowling Alone: America's Declining Social Capital" reports a serious trend of community disengagement.

People don't vote as much as they used to. Attendance at public meetings has fallen by a third between 1973 and 1993, as have involvement in local organizations and involvement in community affairs. Maybe we've become cynical about politics. But other trends suggest a deeper explanation.

We're not attending church as often—church attendance is down by a sixth since the 1960s. PTA membership is half of its 1964 level. Membership in civic and fraternal organizations—such as the Red Cross, Boy Scouts, Lions, Elks, Shriners, and Masons—has dropped.

And although more Americans are bowling than in the past, organized leagues have plummeted in the last decade. Despite a 10 percent increase in total bowlers between 1980 and 1993, league bowling has fallen by 40 percent. Bowling alleys have been hit by this trend, since solo bowlers consume a third of the beer and pizza as league bowlers. Profits in bowling come from food, not alley fees.

Putnam explored several explanations for this loss of civic participation—the movement of women into the labor force, increased mobility in the community, fewer children, and the technological transformation of leisure. The most likely answer: television. The time we now waste watching the tube was once invested in the community.

Same goes for computer use . . . the addictive nature of the Internet takes our time and energy away from more communal activities. Like a powerful drug, the Internet snatches our minds from our homes, transporting us into the nowhereville of cyberspace, where time and place have no meaning.

Putnam sees the effects of electronic interactions on society at large. For a view of how this affects the individual, there's psychologist Kimberly Young's groundbreaking study of Internet use, *Caught in the Net*. She showed that 97 percent of Internet users spend longer periods of time on-line than they intended.

Dr. Young tells of individuals dropping out of real-world activities as they invest more time on longer on-line sessions. A skier in Utah doesn't go to the slopes anymore, preferring to spend winter weekends on-line. One worker on a Michigan assembly line no longer goes bowling with the guys from his plant . . . preferring to spend nights flirting on America On-line or searching out cybersex on the Internet.

Raymond, an avid golfer, no longer plays with his pals on Sunday morning—he's too busy talking about golf over the network. Spending evenings behind his monitor, he hardly sees his six-and four-year-old daughters.

Hideotoshi Kato, director of the Japanese Institute of Multimedia Education, reports on the disappearance of what was once called "family togetherness." Now that each family member has a separate television, families no longer gather together in the living room.

The Internet, of course, isn't a family activity. Warm advertising promotions often show parents and children happily clustered around a computer screen. Such Norman Rockwell views of the wired family are lies: Only one person can interact with a computer at any time. Onlookers get bored.

As the Internet augments television, it's hard to believe that citizens will become more involved in neighborhoods. No need to attend a PTA meeting; just post your comments to the school's Web page. No reason to volunteer at the Rotary Club; visit their bulletin board instead. And why go bowling when you've just downloaded a cool new version of Myst?

As the Internet provides customized entertainment, there's even less reason to get involved in the community. Bill Gates writes, "We'll use the personal computer more and more to find people to do social activities with." I bet otherwise: The personal computer works symbiotically with television to eat up our free time.

The costs of computers show up across society: a dumbed-down workforce which can interact with computers but can't deal with the problems of flesh and blood customers. Catalog ordering departments where representatives take orders but cannot answer questions about products. Minimum wage cashiers who scan bar codes but can't make change without a computer. In the holy names of efficiency and speed, we've devalued manual dexterity, mental agility, and social skills.

Meanwhile, our electronic activities cause us to lose interest in—and time for—the very lifeblood of our communities. We're becoming a nation of isolates.

An empowering technology? After watching my life dribble out my modem, I realize the Internet doesn't empower. It enfeebles.

Help! I'm Stuck
at a Help Desk!

Everyone grouses about help lines and support desks. Incessant busy signals. Interminable music-on-hold. Incomprehensible voice-mail menus. Incompetent answers.

For a moment, think about the guy on the other end. I spent a year behind a computer help desk, at Lawrence Berkeley National Laboratory, where I handled walk-ups and phone calls, occasionally making office visits.

Our lab had more than its share of professors and post-docs . . . they'd hide behind cyclotrons and pop up for free cookies at seminars. Turns out that Ph.D. physicists can ask stupid questions, just like everyone else. Someone would ask how to plug in their terminal; next guy might want to differentiate some orthogonal polynomials. I'd handle 'em both, pleased when I could give 'em the right answer, queasy when I didn't know. Gave me a whole new respect for reference librarians.

At the time, my most common query sounded something like, "Help! I'm working against a deadline and I've got to get this report out. How do I change the margins?" Hardly rocket science . . . I'd find out what program they're using—Unix editor, word processor, graphics program, or spreadsheet. Then I'd explain the magic of margins: "First, you move the mouse over to the 'Format' menu. Then hold down the mouse button and move the mouse so the cursor points to 'document.' Now click on the left margin entry and type the left margin width in inches. Click on the right margin entry . . ."

Halfway through the explanation, my caller would interrupt. "Wait. You lost me. Go over that again." I'd start over, and sometimes he'd say, "Don't give me a set of rules. Just tell me how to change the margins."*

Uh oh. I'm dealing with someone who's smart, but who can't follow a logical sequence of rules. We'd bounce back and forth; eventually he'd get the margins right. Two weeks later, he'd call back and sheepishly ask the same question.

Why can I understand margin-changing without cracking a manual, yet some secretaries and nuclear physicists are baffled? It has to do with rules.

People who hate computers have a hard time following someone else's thought rules. Oh, they may be good at follow-

---

* Don't think this is an idiotic question—setting margins can be infuriating when using professional page layout systems like TeX or many Web publishing programs.

ing rules of the road, a recipe for chocolate chip cookies, or an experiment on the cyclotron. But they don't like to solve mental problems by conforming to the instructions of another person. They want to develop their own instructions, invent their own ways of solving problems.

Remember, software is nothing more than an elaborate series of rules. Occasionally undocumented and rigorously enforced computer programs are just huge collections of logical instructions, typically written by programmers on a deadline.

If you're good at understanding the thought-rules of a committee in Redmond, Washington, well, you'll have an easy time with the latest version of Windows.

But some people have a hard time rigorously following rules for thinking which are laid out by others. They're the ones filling the helplines.

What do you call someone who doesn't follow someone else's rules for thought? These are the original thinkers. For the essence of creativity is the refusal to imitate another person's thinking.

Computers hinder those who are unwilling or unable to simply copy another's rubric for solving problems. Those who invent their own tools. Those who make their own pathways.

Who's most frustrated with their computers? Often, it's the original thinkers. The inventive. The creative.

My time behind the counter makes me wonder . . . what kind of questions do non-high-tech companies receive from customers? For example, there's an 800 number on the side of

Tide detergent—does anyone really call to ask, "How do I use laundry soap?"

So I called Procter & Gamble one Monday afternoon to find out how to use Tide detergent. After the usual confused telephone menu, I reached a friendly voice, and I asked what kind of questions she fields. "We get all kinds of questions about our products," she told me. "Whether it's okay to mix dark laundry with whites (it isn't), how much detergent to add in a front loader (half a cup), what temperature is best for washing jeans (cold)."

"But those answers are listed on the side of the box," I said. "Why not just tell someone to read the instructions?"

As it turns out, she's happy when someone calls with those kinds of questions—they're on her cue card. It apparently covers things like "Why is Tide the best detergent?" or "Where can I purchase the giant-sized box?"

What throws her are the questions from outer space. Like why Tide sponsors one TV show but not another. Or the college student writing a chemistry paper, who asks about organic surfactant interactions.

Then there are the abusers. A friend of mine works at Land's End, handling phone sales. She reports that crazies use catalog ordering departments as a low-cost substitute for sex chat telephone lines. Seems that they field several breathers a night—enough to keep a nix list of nuts' phone numbers.

Despite these operational problems, telephone help lines must benefit somebody—they're available for all sorts of products. Kraft Cheese has a support line—do people call asking how to eat Velveeta? Sylvania's lights come with a toll-free help line, just in case you don't know which direction to screw in a light bulb. I called and the guy at the other end coolly informed me that a lumen was a measure of a light's brightness, a watt was how much electricity the lamp consumed, and no, he didn't know any lightbulb jokes.

Which leads me to imagine what it must be like running a support desk for the Ford Motor Company:

"Hello, I've got a problem with my new car."

"Sure, what's up?"

"Well, it won't move. It worked great for a few days and then it stopped. Hasn't moved since."

"Well, did it stop all by itself?"

"Yep. I was driving down Highway 24, right near the Claremont exit, when I saw a billboard advertising some kind of pest eradicator with a giant blue mouse. Well, right there—poof!—it just stopped. Just like that."

"You mean your car just stopped?"

"Yeah, just like I told you. Couldn't have been more'n a hundred feet away from the mouse. It wouldn't start."

"Uh, how long since you added gas?"

"Gas?"

"You know, gasoline. The stuff you put in the tank."

"You have to put gas in it? Are you sure? After all, this is a new car . . ."

Does Boeing supply a toll-free number with every aircraft sold? Since they're located down the road from Microsoft, maybe they could share the same help desk:

"Welcome to the Microsoft and Boeing Consumer Support Line automated service. Please press 1 for important upgrade information. Press 2 if you have a start-up problem. Press 3 if the variostatic grommet has loosened on the leading edge aerelon. Press 4 if your product has crashed . . ."

The Connected Library

andi Webb, a councilperson in Simi Valley, California, wants to close the community library system: "We need to rip out those useless bookcases, filled with outdated books that are seldom opened, and replace them with low-cost computers and CD-ROMs and high-speed Internet access lines."

Yee-haw! Computers will eliminate those pesky libraries. Get rid of them books. After the book-burning festival, let's eliminate local politicians, now that computers and telephones let us instantly vote on issues.

Alongside churches and day-care centers, libraries are about the most underfunded and underappreciated of our society's institutions. The field receives so little respect that library schools are changing their names to "schools of information management." Apparently embarrassed by their lack of status, many librarians now call themselves information specialists.

Of course, practically every person is an information specialist. A baker specializes in information about breads and cakes. A historian is certainly an information specialist. So is a doctor. Taxicab drivers, too. "Information specialist" is a meaningless, generic title.

I may not know what an information specialist does, but I sure know what a librarian oughta do. For two millennia, they've been stewards of books, charged with organizing, cataloging, preserving, and making books available. Our cornucopia of historical appreciation, technological progress, and cultural awareness isn't the result of a team of information specialists; rather it's due to centuries of rarely thanked librarians.

Yet as librarians turn away from their heritage and toward computers, our book collections become less well preserved, less organized, and less available. Their name change symbolizes a transformation of librarians from stewards of our cultural endowment to professional information handlers. They're now at home answering e-mail, reading Internet mailing lists, and surfing the Web. Can't blame them: I'd rather check out some Usenet scuttlebutt than deal with a confused patron at the reference desk.

Libraries, of course, are riding the information age bandwagon. With great fanfare, the University of California opened their version of the library of the future, a brand-new library facility. The official reason for moving the library was seismic strengthening—Berkeley's in earthquake territory and someone worried about books falling off shelves. But pretty quickly, the library reconstruction got hijacked by library automation folks. These are information management types—typically with degrees in computer science—who feel they know more about how libraries should be run than librarians.

The old friendly library of stacks and study tables morphed into an information-age monolith, sprouting hundreds of computers. A cumbersome spiral staircase showcases the importance of appearance over function. It's admired by administrators, architects, and technologists. Of course—they don't have to use it.

To make room for the computers and spiral staircase, half the books were shipped ten miles off campus, into a book warehouse. The books available at the actual library are just an echo of the entire collection. Sandi Webb's wishes have come true: Any book that hasn't been checked out in a year gets warehoused. Thus, there's a complete set of Tom Clancy novels on the shelf, but if you're searching for anything over twenty years old, your book has to be hauled in on tomorrow's bus.

And don't think that you can go to the warehouse to read. You'll discover that you can't browse the shelves—books aren't filed by subject, title, or author. They're warehoused by size. Perfect for a computer call system. Impossible for the researcher.

Ever hear of a bookshelf that has stopped working? I've witnessed it. To save space, my library put its shelves on rollers, called compact shelving. To get to a book, you turn a wheel and roll several bookshelves, in order to open up an aisle to reach your volume. Nice idea, so long as the mechanism works. When a wheel gets jammed, you can't move the shelves, so your book's out of reach. If several people want books, they wait in line for an aisle to open up. Wait in an aisle next to a bookshelf and nobody can get to any other shelf. It's a storage system designed to provide only the book you're hunting for. Nothing else.

Library administrators love compact shelving; open shelves take up more space than rolling bookcases. Combined with offsite warehousing of books, research libraries are becoming systems which will deliver only the book which you request . . . a fiendish way to prevent both browsing and serendipitous research.

Of course, the big library improvement is universal Internet availability. Not just dozens of workstations. My university's library of the future features four ethernet ports at every table. Sprouting from some study carrels are eight computer ports and sixteen power outlets. Every work space has a high-speed link to the Internet.

These connections let you hook up your laptop computer to the Internet. Of course, you have to supply the computer, cable, software, and account. That's never a problem for the information specialists who'll happily give you a tour.

Who's using all those library ports? At the University of California library, almost nobody. Walking past carrels and tables, I've seen about five students linking their laptops to the network. Practically everyone at the library is reading books. Curiously, all of the library's public terminals are in use—often by students playing Internet games—but the hundreds of computer connections remain unused.

Well, not quite unused. About half of the library ethernet ports have been broken. Some outlets have pencils stuffed into them. Others show broken faceplates or have been pried apart. Many connectors are missing, leaving a rectangular hole and a colorful bouquet of Class-V communications wires.

Maybe I'm seeing the effect of bored students, curious to see how connectors work. Maybe campus lowlifes infest the library, seeking to vandalize pricey computer networks. Perhaps it's the result of a conspiracy of Luddite librarians who object to technology pushing aside their jobs.

Whatever the explanation, so far the electronically wired library has been a dud for students, researchers, and librarians. The only ones who really celebrate this boondoggle are the library automation promoters. They, of course, call it a model for future libraries.

Once, the University of California's library ranked second only to Harvard. But since the library renovation and computerization, the Association of Research Libraries dropped its ranking from second to fifth place. Local librarians feel it will drop another few notches next year, since it is no longer adding as many books as it once did. Sad news for library automation hucksters: College ratings bureaus take into account such outmoded ideas as how many books a library has, how available they are, and the staffing of the library. They don't count unused ethernet ports.

What about public libraries? Worried that I was just considering the needs of researchers, I conducted a spur-of-the-moment, utterly unsystematic survey in Berkeley. I stood on a street corner and asked a dozen passersby, "What do you want in a public library?"

Fully half of those questioned replied, "I don't have any money to give you," and kept walking.

Of the half dozen who took me seriously, the most common answer was "I want books in the library. Lots of books." A few asked for magazines, newspapers, and journals. Several insisted on a good librarian. Evening hours. A harried mom wanted Saturday morning storytelling. Nobody mentioned CD-ROMs, Internet terminals, or multimedia computers.

Yet year after year, as the public library's budget gets cut, they cut down on acquisitions, librarians, and open hours. I find fewer new books, smaller magazine racks, understaffed reference desks, earlier closing times.

But one part of the library budget never seems to get cut: the money spent on CD-ROMs, multimedia software, and network connections. Which is odd, given that these are expensive and quickly become obsolete. And, at least in my limited survey, hardly in demand.

According to a survey in *School Library Journal,* 1994 school expenditures on audiovisual and computer equipment roughly equaled book costs . . . each about five thousand dollars. By 1998, computers were way ahead of books.

For some reason, librarians—oops, I mean information specialists—feel that their library isn't doing a good job unless it has plenty of electronic gizmos and a flashy Web site. American

Library Association conferences hold dozens of sessions on how to make library Web pages. Does this serve library patrons? Local communities? Or does it mainly advertise to distant Internet surfers, who never visit the library and only rarely read books?

Moreover, as librarians get replaced by techno-literate info-specs, you'll find fewer helpful faces behind the library counter. Rhonda Neagle is a library media specialist and technology facilitator at Logan High School in New Haven, California. "It's only the rare moment in any day when I'm on the floor helping kids," she reports. The rest of the time, she's troubleshooting laser printers and VCRs, serving on committees, and overseeing networks, according to the June 1997 *Electronic Learning* magazine.

Rapid obsolescence hits libraries hard. Twenty-five years ago, Fort Worth installed the newest and most expensive computers in their library. The modern replacements cost three million dollars, so they dipped into their endowment. A decade from now, there will be no nest egg to replace the obsolete 1997 computers.

Compare a well-cataloged collection of books, magazines, and newspapers with two dozen high-tech Internet workstations, complete with multimedia software. Which will last longer? Which better serves a neighborhood of children, young adults, adults, and elderly? Which promotes reading, study, and reflection? Which is more likely to be seen as a toy? Which will better preserve our heritage and foster a sense of scholarship and friendship?

Library bureaucrats adopt a gee-whiz attitude toward the Internet: "Libraries must develop a new paradigm," writes Brown University library administrator Brian Hawkins. He wants more computers, more networks, and fewer books.

Meanwhile, librarians politely yawn at traditional library tasks, such as cataloging works, storing books, and staffing reference desks. Berkeley's library committee seeks a "fundamental shift in emphasis from being a warehouse to becoming a gateway for information." Translation: Give 'em computers and get rid of books.

The result of this technolust is that libraries—public and private—are hiring lots of computer specialists. Meanwhile, they're laying off librarians. They're spending money on new databases, but not new books. There's no librarian to help you figure out the thousands of available databases. Gateway to information, indeed.

It's odd to read articles in *Forbes* and *Fortune* on how information is the career of the future. Yet librarians, who have taken care of information for millennia, can't find jobs.

During the 1960s, libraries spent zillions on what was then new media: 16mm films, phonograph records, and filmstrips. Then, as now, the stuff was expensive, quickly went out of date, and tough to archive. What happened to all those phonograph records purchased by your library in 1965?

Today, the closest thing we have to a digital archive medium is the CD-ROM. Yet it has a life span of thirty to fifty years. Within a few decades, newer devices will make CD-ROM readers obsolete. And when manufacturers no longer build reading devices, libraries won't be able to access their collection of CD-ROMs. They'll wind up in landfill.

But a book? It's universally accessible, easily stored, immediately readable, completely portable.* Thousands of years have demonstrated the book's importance and permanence.

And that's what the high-tech library reformers are out to gut. As librarians get laid off, branches run understaffed. They're open perhaps one or two nights a week. They don't subscribe to out-of-town papers. They quietly cancel story hours. Instead of a librarian helping you look up a book, you're pointed to a computer.

Our technologists are working to change our libraries into sterile information warehouses, filled with workstations yet devoid of books. What'll happen when the Internet is universally available and nobody needs to visit the library to search for information? Will libraries close up because trendy "information gateway" grants aren't available and they no longer have any books?

I can't think of a more effective way to eliminate libraries. Burning books won't work—centuries of fanatics, censors, and dictators have tried and failed. And you can't close down libraries by political fiat: They're far too popular in neighborhoods.

No, the best way to gut our libraries is to ship the books off to distant warehouses, supplant librarians with generic information specialists, and replace bookshelves with gleaming com-

---

* For a really permanent media archive, carve your message into turtle shells and sheep bones, and pass them along to oracles at the royal court. Or paint pictures onto cave walls with berry juice.

puter workstations. Donate computers and software which will quickly become obsolete. Provide patrons with CD-ROMs and high-speed Internet ports. Encourage kids to surf the Web rather than read books. Count hits on your Web page instead of visitors to the stacks. Pretty soon, traffic to the stacks will evaporate and the library will fossilize.

In the struggle for liberty and literacy, books and libraries are the best weapons we've got. Use them. Appreciate them. Support them.

Planned Obsolescence

At best, computers seem to have a five-year life span. Yesterday's speedy system winds up in today's landfill. A once modern 486 microprocessor draws sneers previously reserved for mechanical typewriters. Programs won't run on the old dinosaurs. You can't get batteries for a seven-year-old laptop.

Aah, planned obsolescence! Way back in the 1950s, keeping up with the Joneses meant purchasing a new car every other year. The auto companies passed off new models by adding sleek fins, flashy chrome, and two-tone paint jobs. Minor mechanical improvements were labeled breakthroughs. The old one-toned cars wound up in junkyards, trampled under the relentless march of progress.

Automobile manufacturers developed a system where cars were built to fall apart after a set time. Five years after introducing a model, General Motors would stop selling spare parts. Engine bearings were built to last about forty thousand miles. Standards changed—6 volt electrical systems got bumped to 12.

It wasn't just cars, of course. Radios, washing machines, and office equipment were designed to look modern and fall apart faster. Even vacuum cleaners became streamlined. In 1953, the National Association of Manufacturers published full-page photographs of a kerosene lantern with the caption "It still works, but wouldn't you rather have an electric light?" Their real message, of course, was consumption . . . keep business rolling.

Besides perfectly usable cars, what was lost because of this emphasis on elimination of the old? Well, from 1940 to 1960, some two dozen municipal rail systems were dismantled by oil, tire, and auto companies. Hardly anyone spoke out against this demolition, which resulted in more oil, tires, and cars sold, not to mention longer waits in traffic and suburban congestion.

Through the 1950s, cars steadily improved, although Japanese competition jogged the process more than yearly style changes. Tail fins came and went, as did 450-horsepower V-8 engines and Burma Shave signs.

By 1970, people figured out that it simply wasn't necessary to purchase a new car every couple years. The median age of cars on the road increased from a bit over two years old in 1962 to eight years by 1998. Odometers grew from five to six digits as consumers demanded that their cars last longer than a hundred thousand miles. You replace your car when it stops working, not when Ford brings out self-dimming headlights.

As automobiles shifted from trendsetting items to generic commodities, annual car shows made fewer headlines. Yes, cars continue to evolve, as car makers respond to consumer demand, rather than a perceived two-year buying cycle. Toyota and Ford dealers now stock parts for that ten-year-old sedan.

Today, planned obsolescence has returned with a vengeance. It's a driving force behind the high-tech industry, Computer hardware makers, obsessed with processor speeds, seem to deliver ever faster models about as quickly as General Motors in the 1950s.

Meanwhile, obsolete computers decorate closets of offices and homes. They're perfectly functional but no longer able to run the newest programs or multimedia games. Who knows what happens to previous generations of computers? There's a used car dealership in even the smallest town, but not many used computer stores. One California firm purchases obsolete computers for a little over ten cents a pound. At least when the 1957 Edsel was announced, it wasn't advertised as "turbocharged." Or was it?

But it isn't the hardware alone that quickly grows out of date. Look at the software we're being sold: Every program available today has been updated, enhanced, upgraded, and improved. Programs share the short life of grocery store lettuce.

New software releases inevitably claim to patch bugs, add features, and be even more user friendly. These, of course, are mutually exclusive goals: New features add bugs while making the program more complex to use. And isn't it a bit galling to buy new software simply to correct programming mistakes?

Just as our 1950s ancestors could never quite keep up with the Joneses, today it's impossible to keep up with the latest software releases. Computers are sold with pre-installed programs; within a year at least some of them become obsolete. Within a few years, the disk cries out for updates.

Not that it's enough to install the latest updates. Sadly, we're limited by how much time we can spend learning the newest changes. It's not just that the programs become obsolete—planned or unplanned. We slowly lose our ability to adapt to the river of techno-glop. We can spend our lives constantly upgrading our computers, or we can simply use the systems. Software firms promise painless updates, but most every upgrade swallows at least an afternoon. Even trivial changes may take days to install and debug.

As our programs become increasingly interlinked, it becomes harder for programmers to make important changes. Interfaces and protocols developed over the past decade have become difficult to upgrade without disrupting the many programs in daily use. The inertia of installed software damps the introduction of new.

At the same time, many programs are becoming, well, mature. There's just not much demand for revolutionary new word processors. Kinda hard to get excited about a few new spreadsheet features.

In time, I wonder if developing and installing improvements will become so time-consuming that it'll hardly be worth the effort. It may become easier—and cheaper—to toss out the old computer and start from scratch.

What'll happen to the software industry if the future program releases are greeted with yawns? If nobody lines up to buy Windows 2020? Or if people sit back, contented with their Octium processors, so uninspired that they don't purchase the next leap forward?

Consider the high-tech stocks with stratospheric values. These prices are predicated on strong future earnings. But if fewer people purchase new computers, those share prices—like those of General Motors in the early 1970s—may tumble.

I'm sure that planned obsolescence will find a new home: most likely the World Wide Web. Web sites come and go like champagne bubbles—last week's hot site is today's file-not-found error. Information ages faster than software.

And as information grows dated, Web pages will need constant attention: tuning, updates, and more hyperlinks. All this, of course, demands vigilant human attention. The fountain of free Internet information requires constant maintenance . . . and if consumers aren't willing to pay, the result will be obsolete Web sites with dangling pointers and outdated information.

Come to think of it, human beings—indeed all biological species—are incapable of planned obsolescence. Since we become obsolete without any planning, why should computers be much different? Maybe this explains why the Internet's most common messages are birth cries, "This page under construction" and death moans, "Referenced page not found."

New Uses for
Your Old Computer

As I peer into my cellar of old computers, key-boards, disk drives, and not-fast-enough modems, I realize that high-tech gizmos make pretty bad investments. A car maintains more value over a decade than any computer. Within six years, a two-thousand-dollar computer will be worth about a dollar a pound. Short of a boat anchor, what's to be done with an old computer?

Why, donate it to a school, of course! We'll put the equipment back in service, put kids behind a useful computer, and cut down on landfills. Add in possible tax advantages and everyone wins.

Hardly.

Once I too was pumped up about donating old equipment to schools. But after watching what happened to these clunkers, I've changed my mind.

A year after working with a Berkeley computer user's group, I revisited some of the classrooms where our donated computers had been installed. Most machines had been stuffed into closets or were gathering dust on shelves. Oh, a few were used to play old computer games. One kept track of student grades. Several had disappeared from the school. But none were used in regular scholastic instruction.

What went wrong?

Well, those computers were way old. That's why businesses donated 'em. Students get frustrated by the same things that cause businesses to toss out those old dogs: The disk's too slow, memory's too small, there's no CD-ROM drive. A thirty-year-old radio may still play music, but a ten-year old CPU can't decompress an MP3 track from a punk rock album. We want to get rid of obsolete textbooks in schools. So we give our students obsolete computers. Go figure.

Donated computers never come with documentation, and they're usually missing cables, disk drives, or keyboards. It might take an hour just to figure out the computer's configuration. The better part of a day to make it work properly.

Anyway, the hardware's the easy part. The old software that might run on a 286 class computer simply isn't available . . . the programs were upgraded long ago, and the new versions won't run on old machines.

By donating these digital antiques, we assume that someone at the school will configure, install, and maintain a variety of obsolete computers. It's asking a lot to expect a high school history teacher to fix a ten-year-old computer without documentation or even telephone help.

When typewriters became obsolete, did businesses donate their clunky Smith Coronas to schools?

There's a good reason American corporations donate old computers to schools. They get a tax break. They write off the doorstops and don't have to pay a junkyard. A non-profit foundation resells whatever's usable and passes the unsellable stuff to a school.

On the other hand, at least one company found a way to profit by giving new computers to schools. ZapMe Networks laces the educational computers with advertisements directed at kids. As fifth graders browse the Web, they're targeted with ads directed at ten-year-olds. Under the guise of "encouraging an interactive learning environment that opens up discussion among educators, students, and parents," this company delivers children directly to corporate clients.

Related to this nutty idea of dumping obsolete computers in schools is the annual geekfest called Net Day. Every year, with considerable political fanfare, Internet buffs become do-gooders by wiring schools for Internet access. Businesses—especially phone companies—donate connections and talk about the importance of high-bandwidth connections. President, Vice President, and senators dutifully don gloves to pull wires down high school hallways. Television cameras zoom in on children downloading computer images of rain forest animals.

Nobody asks how these connections fit into the school's curriculum, or whether the students might be better off taking a field trip to the zoo. Nobody asks why so much attention is paid to Net Day, and so little paid to School Library Week. Nobody asks why computer jocks happily visit schools to write Web pages, but rarely show up at PTA meetings. Nobody asks who'll fix the problem when the amateur wiring job breaks. Heck, nobody asks whether the politicians did a good job of installing the wires. Nope, the goal of Net Day is to get those classrooms wired. It's technology for technology's sake.

Not exactly, says Michael E. Kaufman, co-founder of Net Day. Because businesses depend on the Internet, children must understand the technology now if they're to have any hope of finding decent jobs once they graduate. "We have an obligation to prepare kids in education for a successful future," Kaufman says. "Doing that without the technology that they will be called on to use seems shortsighted."

Students won't have any hope of finding decent jobs without knowing the Internet? I'll bet that most businesses would far prefer applicants with creative problem-solving abilities, human interaction skills, and a foreign language, not to mention punctuality, persistence, honesty, and a work ethic. All the things that you can't learn from the Internet.

What about those jobs that Net Day prepares kids for? Internet employment is cyclical, insecure, and often unrewarding. Today's digital sweatshop is a cubicle, with tight deadlines and often no promise of work beyond the end of the month. Rather than employees, businesses hire consultants and contractors—they don't get benefits and are easier to lay off. With so many flocking to the field, and so few profits generated by the Web, simple economics suggests that the day will come when there are few openings available.

By holding the computer as provider of both education and employment, we're grossly overselling technology and causing an absurd overspecialization in our workforce.

The annual Net Day hoopla makes me wonder: What should we do with old TV sets when the long-promised high-definition television makes 'em obsolete? Aha! Donate your obsolete television to a school. They'll use it for education. We can have an annual event to attach TV antennas to schools and to connect them to cable systems. We'll call it TV Day.

If businesses are really looking for ways to improve classrooms with technology, give every teacher a photocopier. It's cheap—half the cost of a computer. Easy to use. Every teacher I've met would love to have a copier to distribute materials in class. If it breaks, no class time is lost. Saves time too: no more treks to the office and queues to make copies.

Or how about donating more communications equipment—say, telephone lines? Hey—school boards justify computers in schools because they're wonderful communications and research tools. So why aren't telephones provided on every student's desk?

Okay, it's absurd to give every student a phone. But how about providing one to every teacher? After all, teachers are about the only professionals in the workplace without a phone on their desks.

Here's why not. After teaching in a high school classroom, I realized that interruptions swallow enormous amounts of class time. Each message over the public address system waylays students' attention and sidetracks your narrative. You then have to get the students back in order and thinking about the lesson. That takes five minutes . . . a tenth of the available class time. Trivial administrative messages feed this stream of classroom disruptions. Essentially any message short of a fire alarm can wait until between classes. Telephones only make classrooms worse.

Far better to cut the wires to classroom intercoms and shut down the public address systems. Instead of pushing more communications into the classroom, we should give teachers the respect of at least not interrupting them while they're practicing their profession. Anything that'll eliminate interruptions is bound to help learning.

There's already an annual turn-off-your-TV week, where schools try to wean kids away from the tube. Perhaps, given the ubiquity of cyberspace, there'll be a turn-off-your-computer week, where kids are encouraged to spend a few nights without reading their e-mail or checking into a chat line. Should the two holidays overlap, families might even spend a few evenings together.

So what should we do with a still-working but obsolete computer? Looking at my ten-year-old Macintosh, I realized that I'd become attached to the old buzzard. Ecological considerations aside, I couldn't bear to toss a friend into the Dumpster.

I switched the ol' Mac on for one last time, and watched the operating system wake up. After a few minutes, the familiar screen saver came to life: a quaint animation of three fish swimming across the Mac's screen. Coarsely rendered in black and white, the cartoon fish were supposed to prevent screen burn-in.

Fish. That's the ticket. How about turning my old Mac into an aquarium? A quick search across the Web turned up plans for a MacQuarium by Andy Inhatko. A zany and utterly irreverent Mac addict, Andy knows the joys of computing and occasionally retrofits computers into fish tanks.

So I invested ten dollars in a couple of pieces of plate glass, some silicone caulk, and a box of Band-Aids. First step is to remove the electronics, cathode-ray tube, and several pieces of plastic. A couple afternoons of cutting, fitting, and cementing glass resulted in two sliced fingers and a working aquarium.

Once belittled as a beige toaster, my Macintosh has been reborn as a two-gallon fish tank. A little gravel and a bubbler complete the illusion: Three happy goldfish now live within my ten-year-old system.* They deliver a far more realistic fish rendering than any screen saver.

So what do I do with my old IBM PC? I popped the top off the cabinet, discarded the motherboard and disk drive, sealed up the holes, and checked for leaks. Now that it resembled a six-inch-deep tray, I placed it on the floor and poured in a pound of Kitty Litter.

My high-tech Kitty Litter box.

* According to Andy, mine are actually koi, which (appropriately) are close relatives of the carp. And having grown too big for the MacQuarium, they've graduated into a pond.

The Plague of PowerPoint

Perhaps you've not yet seen a PowerPoint talk. You soon will.

Imagine a boring slide show. Now add lots of generic, irrelevant, and pyrotechnic graphics. What have you got? A boring slide show, complete with irrelevant whizbang graphics.

Ten years ago, these computer graphics shows seemed futuristic. Today, they're hackneyed. PowerPoint is the enemy of a good talk.

Presentation software goes under several names: PowerPoint, Persuasion, Presentation, or Freelance. Promoted as the up and coming way to reach an audience, it's used by technical speakers, sales folk, instructors, lawyers, and, naturally, politicians.

These programs let anyone make transparencies or video

displays, complete with clipart, fancy backgrounds, and colorful charts. Used with a video projector, your audience can watch text scroll onto the screen accompanied by animated sprites and dancing corporate logos.

Used to be, you'd watch someone stand before an audience and stammer through a talk, cued by index cards and an occasional transparency. The audience scribbled notes and tried not to yawn.

All that's changed, thanks to the convergence of personal computers, video projectors, and laser printers. Today, the lecturer fiddles with a computer, focuses the projector, and adjusts his microphone. He pushes a few buttons and up pops a perfectly laid-out computer graphics display. New graphics appear on command, usually as bullet points perfectly lined up in columns. The audience has been given paper copies of the show in advance, so they read the notes and try not to yawn.

Almost nobody likes to stand up and talk to an audience. Techies, accustomed to dealing with computers rather than people, are especially shy. So naturally they latch onto anything which will insulate them from this experience. In public speaking, PowerPoint is the coward's choice.

Once, foibles, yarns, and a few jokes sympathetically linked speaker to audience. Now, everyone's either staring at the video screen or reading their handouts. The speaker becomes an incidental accessory behind the lectern.

Not that the speaker cares. He's too busy fiddling with buttons and watching the screen. With his back to the audience, the orator knows what the next slide will say, as does the audience. Should he forget a line or head off on a tangent, the program prompts him back to the prepared talk.

Result: a predictable, pre-programmed, pre-produced lecture, devoid of any human content. The audience might as well watch a videotape.

Sure, meetings are notoriously tedious. And anything that can jazz 'em up is welcome. But PowerPoint and its cousins seem destined to make meetings even more boring.

This assumes that the electronics go right. If the computer hangs up, the software crashes, or the video projector flakes out, the speaker's cooked. He'll likely fumble with the cables or call for a technician. All of which wastes five or ten minutes and incompletely derails his talk. I've watched it happen.

Oh, I admire the technical capabilities of these programs. With the right hookup, you can link to a Web site or copy graphs from a spreadsheet. You can include sound effects, cartoons, and clipart. But a hundred people have gathered to connect with a speaker, not to watch a light show.

What motivates an audience? Emotion. Passion. Fire. A sense of warmth, excitement, shared adventure. A PowerPoint-driven meeting delivers chilly, pre-programmed video graphics. You see graphs, numbers, and bullet charts. But dancing sprites and flashing logos can't inspire zeal, loyalty, outrage, or a clarion call to action.

The computer-generated graphics draw the crowd's attention. Rather than watching you, the audience gazes at the fonts and animation. They're already holding your handouts, so there's no reason to take notes or intently listen for your important points. Indeed, since everything's on the screen and in the handouts, there's not much reason to listen to what you say.

We remember the performance, not a font or logo. We want to identify with the speaker, but it's hard to overcome the sterility of the computer graphics. When was the last time you saw an inspiring multimedia show? When was the last meeting where you said, "Hey, those glitzy graphics sure impressed me!"

I can imagine Abraham Lincoln at Gettysburg, sporting a video projector and PowerPoint. He'd show a graphic of eighty-seven calendars flipping by, fading into an animation of Washington crossing the Delaware. Highlighted on his bullet chart would be the phrases "A new nation," "Conceived in liberty," and "All men are created equal."

If only PowerPoint were confined to computer conferences, where it would just put techies to sleep. Alas, it's now showing up in schools. I sat through an American history class dulled by PowerPoint. The high school students sat glassy-eyed as their teacher read the text rolling up the screen. "Warren Harding was the twenty-ninth President and was born in Marion, Ohio. The five most important features of his administration were . . ." Deadly.

Kids latch onto this new way to slack off. A high school student from Wilsonville, Oregon, writes this ungrammatical analysis: "I wasn't doing crap for a presentation that I had to do in class. But I still received a good grade because it was on a Powerpoint stack that took me a half hour to make. There was others in the class that worked their butts off to memorize their presentation, and here am I up there just reading off my presentation that was being projected on the screen."

So it looks as if PowerPoint is fast becoming the replacement for the educational slide show. Just about as relevant. Just about as interesting.

Want to make a splash at your next public talk? Know your material so well that you can speak off the cuff, without computer, laser pointer, or video projector. Scribble your important points on a chalkboard and emphasize them with your voice. Face your audience, not that computer monitor.

Throw out that tired clipart and the clichés about the explosion of technology, the challenge of the future, and the crisis in education. Let me hear your voice, not a pre-programmed sound effect. Show me your ideas, not someone else's template.

Amaze me with your stories. Thrill me with your experiences. Astound me with your brilliance. Convince me with your passion. Show excitement. Intrigue. Anything—just don't bore me with another computer graphics presentation.

I can't help mentioning the Evangelical Church of PowerPoint. At St. John's Lutheran Church in Oxnard, California, worshippers face a multimedia video screen above the altar. Complemented by a thirty-two-channel sound system, PowerPoint projects Picasso-style caricatures onto the screen, along with the high points of the sermon. It can project Internet video clips along with reminders of next week's potluck dinner. And the $160,000 system probably saves several hundred dollars' worth of hymnals.

This is no new-age church—St. John's is a member of the

conservative Lutheran Missouri Synod. Nor is it some isolated foolishness: Other churches are quickly installing computer video systems, including the Camarillo Jubilee Church.

Pastor Mark Beyer says that video projection of his message lets him reach out to the congregation's ears and eyes. "We're just trying to use the tools of the present," he says. "I'd like to use Smell-o-Vision if I could."

Today's omnipresent tool is the Internet: I wonder if Pastor Beyer will develop a Web site where you click on an icon and effortlessly receive enlightenment. No need to show up at church at all.

One Sunday, Pastor Beyer asked his congregation to raise their hands and sing to God. Then he turned and joined his parishioners in looking up at the giant computer display. If God had retained the same sense of outrage he displayed in Daniel 5:25, they'd have seen the flashing message "Mene, Mene, Tekel Upharsin." Instead, the venerated PowerPoint screen answered the supplicants with the message:

"For thou, Lord, art high above all Earth. I exalt thee."

Junk Food and the Internet: The Economics of Information

Information providers inform me that we're building an information superhighway to better work with information processors in the information marketplace. After all, we live in the information-rich information society.

Result? We're overloaded with information. Each day we're reputed to receive two thousand messages, most of them commercial. This barrage anesthetizes our sense of the subtle and further inures us to advertising. How strange, that we respond to this flood by building more channels to feed us still more messages.

But the Internet, for all its promise, doesn't deliver much information—it's mainly a data highway.

Data isn't information. There's a wide gulf between data—

bits, bytes, numbers, and words—and information. Information, unlike data, has accuracy. It's reliable. It's timely. Understandable. Information comes with a pedigree . . . you know the source. Information, unlike data, is useful.

While there's a gulf between data and information, there's a wide ocean between information and knowledge. What turns the gears in our brains isn't information, but ideas, inventions, and inspiration. Knowledge—not information—implies understanding.

And beyond knowledge lies what we should be seeking: wisdom. Sadly, our information society values data over experience, maturity, compassion, and enlightenment.

For while information may be useful, it's generally not valuable. Yes, timely, accurate, important information can be worth a fortune. But the vast bulk of information is valueless. What's the difference between worthless data and useful information? For that matter, what's the economics of information? Despite all that's written about information management, I rarely see much about the value of information.

Like everyone else, I want a sandwich rather than a recipe, a shirt rather than a pattern, and a house rather than a blueprint. Yet cybernauts insist that information carries value. After all, a bank balance is but a collection of numbers. It's a bit like saying that a river is just a line on a map.

The value of information depends on its freshness—yesterday's news is like yesterday's lettuce. Too, the value of information depends on its accuracy and reliability. Details of a secret buyout deal might generate a fortune for the inside trader, but only if the details are right. And some information that's worthless to you might be quite valuable to me.

I'm hardly an economist, but the first law of thermodynamics says that you can't get something for nothing. Extend this with common sense and to give the notion that there's no such thing as a free lunch. If you want something of value, you'll have to pay for it.

In everything we buy, whether goods or services, we look for three qualities: fast, good, and cheap. You can get two of these three qualities, but you just can't get all three at once.

Hunting for a cheap, fast food? Just head over to McDonald's. In a hurry for a good meal? Visit a nice restaurant. And there's a way to get cheap, good food . . . home cooking!

But fast food isn't good. Quality restaurants aren't cheap. And that home-cooked meal won't be quick.

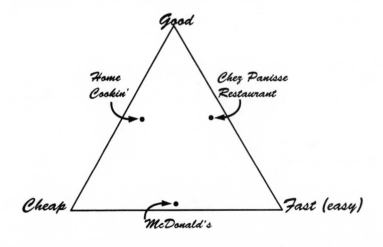

Good, cheap, and fast . . . you can't get all three at once. It applies whether you're buying food, shoes, plumbing, or an education.

It probably even applies to relationships.

It certainly applies to data. If you want quality information cheaply, well, just visit your library. But it won't be fast—you'll have to invest time and energy to uncover exactly what you're looking for.

There are many sources of fast, accurate information as well. Lexis-Nexis and Dow Jones Newswires come to mind—they provide full-text listings of major newspapers, magazines, and research sources. But they're expensive—$50 to $200 an hour.

Want fast, cheap information? Log onto the World Wide Web. It'll travel down the Internet's pipeline as fast as your modem and the network servers. The Internet is the McDonald's of information.

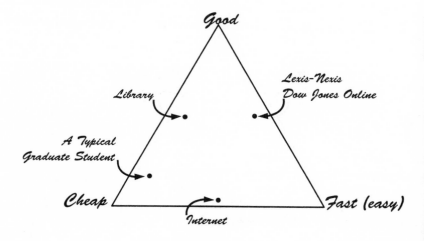

And like McDonald's, the Internet delivers a product which is fast, easy, and cheap. Like McDonald's, it's plenty good enough for many people—it satisfies their needs. And like McDonald's, the Internet drives out classical establishments which deliver high quality. One pushes aside mom-and-pop restaurants; the other undercuts libraries.

George Ritzer, in his book *The McDonaldization of Society,* recognizes that our society has been transformed by a mania for efficiency, predictability, quantification, and control. Hardly surprising to find these to be the strong suits of computing and the Internet, especially in research and education.

What won't you find at McDonald's? At McDonald's, you'll see cooks and counter staff, but not professional chefs or waiters. On the Internet, there are content providers and hot lists, but not professional editors and journalists.

With information, as with food, cheap and fast work against good.

When something is free—like Internet data—its economic worth is practically zero. It's a lesson as old as Adam Smith, yet somehow ignored by those predicting an economic cornucopia from the information age. Free information, like free love, has essentially no value.

The most valuable information—trusted insider tips that can make money—simply aren't available on public networks. Once something's posted on the World Wide Web, it's universally available. The Internet holds no secrets.

Quality in information depends not just on access to raw data. Editors, critics, reviewers, and professional journalists add value. They do so not just by pushing paragraphs around and formatting pages; the main job of an editor is to reject 99 percent of the information reaching her desk.

Most every editor searches for the story that's new, true, important, and well written. Most of what reaches the editor's desk simply doesn't meet these criteria. Whatever else is wrong in journalism and publishing, editors still serve as barometers of literary excellence—paid to recognize what's worth publishing. Paid to spend most of their days saying, "Nope."

Want a world without editors? Just look at the Internet. Anyone can publish there, so naturally, everyone does. The resultant cacophony resembles an ocean of words, with neither meaning nor quality.

"The net represents the ultimate dumbing-down of the computer," writes Ellen Ullman in *Close to the Machine*. "Users seem to believe that they are connected to some vast treasure trove—all the knowledge of our times, an endless digitized compendium, an electronic library of Alexandria—if only they could figure out how to search it properly. They sit and click, and look disconcertedly at the junk that comes back . . . They click 'Back' and 'Back' again, and, like players in a Victorian maze retracing their steps, they emerge to find they are only at the place where they entered."

The Internet's search engines, believed by many to be the answer to their information needs, deliver as much misleading information as they offer useful pointers. Their searches lack depth and breadth: The search engines typically ignore between

60 and 90 percent of all Web pages. Of course, how much of the Internet deserves to be indexed?

Unlike an index or a library, you have to know what you're looking for before you fire up a search engine . . . they don't work with concepts, ideas, or suggestions. And since search engines work with words, you have to know how to spell—and spelling is one of those outdated skills that's no longer taught. Or maybe it's no longer learned.

Computerized search engines are no substitute for a trip to a well-cataloged library. Library catalogers—perhaps the least thanked of a seldom thanked profession—add value to already valuable information. Like indexers, they classify, categorize. And like indexers, theirs is a job that's perceived as easily automated. It ain't so.

Fundamentally, search engines and automated indexing software search for words, not concepts. They know not about language nuances and context. Indeed, consultants commonly tell Web writers to write with a particular structure so that search engines will pick up their points. How odd—organize and communicate our thoughts so that they're easily parsed by a machine. It's as absurd as writing a book to please your indexer.*

Ouch! A human indexer, too, does far more than simply categorize. She interprets. Looks for meaning. Provides context, cross-references, weaves diverse threads into easily searched en-

---

* "I sure wish you would," said ace indexer Nancy Mulvany as she assembled the last few pages of this book.

tries. She digs out concepts, rather than scanning for words. She offers readers handholds into the text. Her job is made easy by highly structured documents, where there's lots of white space and important points come boldfaced. Mechanical indexing software, too, works great for the easy stuff. But tying together subtle points and themes—bringing value to text—is the sole province of the human indexer.

Those with *valuable* information naturally don't upload it to the net . . . they want to be paid for their work. Texas Instruments, for example, explicitly tells its employees not to hand out technical advice over the Usenet news groups—they may be helping a competitor. Would a doctor diagnose medical problems for free over the Internet? What patient would trust such advice? Would an author give away a work if a publishing house was willing to pay to put it into print?

There's another reason why the Internet is such an ocean of mediocrity. Few users are willing to pay for quality over the net. As soon as you charge a fee to enter a Web site, traffic plummets. Apparently, the main way to make money on-line is via advertising. There are more billboards on the Internet than on all the highways in America. While I do find an occasional nugget buried in a ton of dross, vast stretches of the World Wide Web are little more than monuments of narcissism or commercial self-promotions.

Today, the cost of electronic communications is dropping while the price of paper skyrockets. Low-quality information—however you define it—winds up on-line, while the highest-quality ideas find their way onto paper.

As a result, those with important stories to tell will seek to get them in print—it's the medium of quality information. Michael Koenig and Toni Harrell wrote an article about the advantages to on-line publishing, yet they waited a year to have it appear in *Science Magazine,* so that it could be widely read and cited. Stephen Harter studied electronic journals and found that they just don't have much effect . . . apparently, researchers prefer to publish on paper. Which looks more impressive on a résumé: a Web page locator or a string of published papers? If electronic publishing is so central to the future, why don't authors upload their books to the net?

Another question: If Internet communications and interactive video systems are so effective, why do computer enthusiasts flock like lemmings to computer conventions? By and large, they're the ones with the sophisticated gear and high-bandwidth links to the World Wide Web . . . of all people, they should be satisfied with virtual meetings and cyberconventions.

Video conferences are continually promoted as a speedy, cheap way to handle business communications. Yet if they're so effective, why do so many salespeople fly out to meet clients and customers? Similarly, businesses wire their offices for instant e-mail, but most decisions still take place in face-to-face meetings.

Salespeople, intent on closing a deal, realize that e-mail and video conferences cannot replace the myriad ways we communicate ideas and feelings in a physical visit. Speakers and musicians, whose livelihood depends on the electricity of a live audience, can't deliver the thrill of a live performance over the Internet. And in each of our lives, I suspect, the most important, most decisive, and most memorable interactions take place in person.

No electronic bit stream can replace the trust implicit in a handshake or the warmth of an embrace. In communications, as in education, the cheapest way to present facts is often the least memorable and least convincing.

The Internet may be cheap, fast, and easy, but electronic interactions simply aren't as good as face to face. In information, as in food, housing, and schooling, you get what you pay for.

Rule Number Two

Seems that everyone's searching for three things: A great place to live. A terrific job. A wonderful relationship. Well, after years of research, I finally found how to get all three.

Want to make big money in a Wall Street IPO? Looking to jump-start a stagnant career? Searching for the best way to build a relationship? Hunting for a rent-stabilized apartment in Manhattan? Need to balance the federal budget without raising taxes? Yearning for a Nobel prize or the cure to pattern baldness?

There's a surprisingly easy answer—just apply Arthur Bisguier's Rule Number Two.

Sure, there are plenty of self-help books, like Sun-Tzu's *Art of War,* Machiavelli's *The Prince,* or Dale Carnegie's *How to Win Friends and Influence People.* But whenever I'm in doubt—and that's rather often—I apply Rule Number Two.

You see, Arthur Bisguier plays chess. No, he's not just some run-of-the-mill chessmonger—he's a grand master. An international grand master. At seventy years old, he's a member of the U.S. Chess Hall of Fame and has played more people than any other grand master. He probably rubs pawns with the likes of Bobbie Fischer and Boris Spassky. And he's going to show me— and you—how to always win at chess!

All you need to know to master chess is contained in Bisguier's short but subtle booklet *Ten Tips to Winning Chess*. It's available free from the U.S. Chess Federation.

Now here's the best part: His revolutionary method works in a greater context . . . Bisguier's formula for winning at chess can be profitably applied to almost every crisis in life. Whether strategic or tactical, whenever you're confused, just reach for Rule Number Two.

So how do you win at chess?

Page through Bisguier's pamphlet . . . There, over on page 9, is the secret to winning at chess. When in doubt—whether in chess or in life—just follow Rule Number Two.

Make the best possible move.

---

1. Look at your opponent's move.

☞ 2. **Make the best possible move.**

3. Have a plan.

4. Know what the men are worth.

Makes sense to me.

isolated by the internet

For all my grinching about the soul-deadening effects of the Internet, most Internet users speak positively about it. One friend tells how she found a support group for an obscure medical condition. Another tells me that his modem provides an escape from a dull world, providing a rich mixture of fantasy and role playing. One soon-to-be-married couple writes how they met through postings to a Usenet news group. And one computer programmer confesses that although she's extremely shy in person, in her electronic chat room, she becomes a feisty, enchanting contessa. Meanwhile wired families keep in touch via e-mail, and new friendships blossom thanks to on-line special interest groups. Isolated hobbyists sign onto Web sites to exchange information and help each other. Surely the electronic virtual community is a positive social development.

Well, not necessarily. According to Carnegie Mellon University psychologists Robert Kraut and Vicki Lundmark, there are serious negative long-term social effects, ranging from depression to loneliness. The result of a concerted research effort, their findings were surprising since this research was funded by high-tech firms like AT&T, Apple Computer, Lotus, Intel, and Hewlett Packard. Their report, "The Internet Paradox—A Social Technology That Reduces Social Involvement and Psychological Well-Being?" appeared in the September 1998 issue of the *American Psychologist.*

Kraut and Lundmark had asked how using the Internet affects connections between people. They looked at both the extent and the depth of human links, and tried to understand how the Internet affected these connections. Deep social ties are relationships with frequent contact, deep feelings of involvement, and broad content. Weak ties have superficial and easily broken bonds, infrequent contact, and narrow focus. Weak ties link us to information and social resources outside our close local groups. But it's the strong social ties that buffer us from stress and lead to better social interactions.

Hardly surprising that strong personal ties come about when you're in close proximity to someone . . . it's been that way for millennia. Suddenly, along comes the Internet, reducing the importance of distance and letting you develop new relationships through chat rooms, e-mail, news groups, and Web pages.

To learn about the social effects of the Internet, Kraut and Lundmark followed ninety-six families of various backgrounds for two years. They provided computers, software, modems, accounts, and training; in all, some 256 individuals entered the study, and two thirds of them completed it. The software allowed full Internet use, but recorded how much time was spent in various on-line activities. Each participant answered questionnaires before they went on-line, after a year, and after two years of Internet use.

The researchers measured stress, loneliness, and depression using standardized psychological tests like the UCLA Loneliness Scale and the Center for Epidemiologic Studies Depression Scale. Participants would agree or disagree with statements like "I feel everything I do is an effort," "I enjoy life," "I can find companionship when I want it," "There is someone I could turn to for advice about changing my job or finding a new one." Kraut and Lundmark then measured each participant's social circle and distant social network during the two-year study.

After following the study group, the psychologists found an average increase in depression by about 1 percent for every hour spent on-line per week. On-line activity resulted in increased loneliness as well. On the average, subjects began with sixty-six members in their nearby social circle. For every hour each week spent on-line, this group shrank by about 4 percent.

Depression. Loneliness. Loss of close friendships. This is the medium that we're promoting to expand our global community?

It's true that many on-line relationships developed as well, but most represented weak social ties rather than deep ones: a woman who exchanged mittens with a stranger, a man who exchanged jokes with a colleague he met over a tourist Web site. A few friendships blossomed—one teenager met his prom date on-line—but these were rarities. And even though such friendships were welcomed when they happened, there was an overall decline in real-world interaction with family and friends.

The overwhelming majority of on-line friendships simply aren't deep. On-line friends can't be depended on for help with tangible favors: small loans, baby-sitting, help with shopping, or advice about jobs and careers. One participant "appreciated the e-mail correspondence she had with her college-aged daughter, yet noted that when her daughter was homesick or depressed, she reverted to telephone calls to provide support."

Kraut and Lundmark concluded that "greater use of the Internet was associated with small, but statistically significant declines in social involvement as measured by communication within the family and the size of people's local social networks, and with increases in loneliness, and depression. Other effects on the size of the distant social circle, social support, and stress did not reach standard significance levels but were consistently negative." Paradoxically, the Internet is a social technology used for communication, yet it results in declining social involvement and psychological well-being.

What's important to remember is that their research wasn't a collection of casual claims, but "an extremely careful scientific study," said Tora Bikson, a senior scientist at Rand Corporation. "It's not a result that's easily ignored." Despite a decade of concerns, it's the first time that professional psychologists have done such a longitudinal study.

"We were shocked by the findings, because they are counterintuitive to what we know about how socially the Internet is being used," said Dr. Kraut, who hypothesized that Internet use is "building shallow relationships, leading to an overall decline in feeling of connection to other people."

Not surprisingly, computer makers scoffed: One Intel psychologist replied that "This is not about the technology, per se; it's about how it is used. It points to the need for considering social factors in terms of how you design applications and services for technology." In other words, technology is just a neutral tool and social technologists will solve this problem. Uh, right.

According to computer scientists James Katz and Philip Aspden, there's no reason to be pessimistic about the social effects of Internet use. They telephoned six hundred Internet users, to survey the social effects of computer use. Their 1997 report, "A Nation of Strangers," argues that the Internet augments existing communities. It's a medium for creating friendships and to stay in touch with family members. They cheerily suggest that some two million new meetings have taken place thanks to the Internet. Katz and Aspden happily conclude that "The Internet is creating a nation richer in friendships and social relationships."

Unfortunately, Katz and Aspden used a biased system of self-reporting, a phone survey in which those called judged themselves on whether they had gained or lost friends. Hardly anyone's going to tell a stranger on the phone, "Oh, I've lost friends because I spend too much time on-line." Also, while Katz and Aspden tallied all social ties made over the Internet, they didn't probe into the possible loss of strong local ties. Since they didn't ask about the depth, nature, or quality of on-line "friendships," naturally their phone survey delivered a happily optimistic conclusion.

Psychologists point out that the best predictor of psychological troubles is a lack of close social contacts. There's a surprisingly close correlation between social isolation and such problems as schizophrenia and depression. Long hours spent on-line undercut our local social support networks; this isolation promotes psychological troubles.

Kraut and Lundmark's work points to a serious problem looming for wired generations: Will the proliferation of shallow, distant social ties make up for the loss of close local links?

Stanford psychology professor Philip Zimbardo has part of the answer. Since the mid-1970s, he's studied the psychology of shyness. In 1978, Dr. Zimbardo found that some 40 percent of undergraduates said, "I think of myself as shy." By 1988, this number had reached 45 percent. And by 1995, some 50 percent of undergrads saw themselves as shy; some research suggests that 60 percent of the population now suffers from shyness.

Why this epidemic of shyness? At a 1997 conference, Professor Zimbardo pointed to several reasons, many connected to technology. Television and computing make us more passive . . . and passivity feeds into shyness. Now that many family members have separate televisions, watching TV is no longer a communal experience, but rather an isolated, non-social non-encounter. One report suggested that parents, busy from work which they've brought home, spend only six to eight minutes a day talking with their children.

"The electronic revolution of e-mails and faxes means the medium has finally become the message," said Professor Zimbardo. "With more virtual reality overtaking real reality, we're losing ordinary social skills and common social situations are becoming more awkward."

Yep, for better or worse, the only way to learn how to get along with others is to spend plenty of time interacting with people. E-mail, telephones, and faxes all prevent us from learning basic skills of dealing with people face to face. These electronic intermediaries dull our abilities to read each other's gestures and facial expressions, to express our feelings, to strike up conversations with strangers, to craft stories, to tell jokes.* Those weaned on computer communications won't learn basic social rules of conversation. How to interrupt. How to share time with another. How to speak to an audience. When to be quiet.

In the past, shyness has been passed off as a trivial problem that children grow out of. "Although we think of shy people as passive and easily manipulated, at the same time there is a level

* Once, people told stories—you'd pay attention to the homegrown comedian who knew how to tell a joke. Joke telling meant timing, inflection, and expression. Now, thanks to jokes passed by e-mail and Internet forums, stale comedy routines constantly circulate on-line. People who can't tell jokes won't shut their mouths.

of resentment, rage and hostility," Zimbardo warned. I wonder if that explains some of the anger pervading the anonymous chat rooms and postings to Usenet news groups.

The notion that people can become addicted to the Internet was scoffed at by professional psychologists. It was considered to be a joke in the same way that alcoholism, compulsive gambling, and obsessive shopping were thought laughable in the 1950s. After all, you can just stop. Only recently have a few psychologists asked questions about the seductive nature of the Internet and the type of person likely to become hooked. They're finding that the clinical definitions of established addictions fit the profiles of plenty of people who spend their lives on-line.

Psychologist Kimberly Young was among the first to investigate clinical cases of Internet addiction. She tells of a Pennsylvania college student she calls Steve who's on-line sixty to seventy hours a week. Steve's a wizard in the Multi-User Dungeons; Internet fantasy games best known as MUDs.

"MUDs are like a religion to me, and I'm a god there. I'm respected by all the other MUDders . . . Even when I'm not playing, I wonder if there will be more newbies for me to kill that night or which other guys will be playing. I am in control of my character and my destiny in this world. My character is a legend and I identify with him." Yet when Steve's not on-line, he's held back by low self-esteem. Shy and awkward around people, he's uncomfortable around women and believes he doesn't fit in at school. "When I'm playing the MUDs, I'm not feeling lonely or mopey. I'm not thinking about my problems . . . I want to stay on the MUDs as long as I possibly can."

Where once Steve would have work within the real world and slowly learn how to deal with people, today he is able to turn to the Internet for solace and escape.

Compounding the withdrawal of individuals from their close social circle, technology also blurs the line between work and play. Thanks to telephones, pagers, and cell phones, work seeps into our private time, forcing shallow, impersonal communication into quiet hours and intimate moments. E-mail reaches our desktops and laptops; even our wristwatches have alarms and electronic reminders. At home, on the road, or on the golf course, we can't escape an electronic bombardment.

Walking in Yosemite Park, I met a hiker with all the latest paraphernalia hanging from his belt: pager, GPS locator, and electronic altimeter. Amid the quiet of the sugar pines, his cell phone squawked and I overheard one side of his conversation with some New York advertising firm: "Tell both clients that I won't be able to make Monday's meeting," he told an unseen secretary. "I'll get them a proposal when I'm over this cold."

Here's a guy who's brought the stress of his office into the tranquillity of the forest. He's never lost and always in reach. At the same time, he's utterly lost and out of touch.*

Office work tags along with homes equipped with fax ma-

---

* In response to the noise and interruptions, one Japanese symphony hall has installed special transmitters to disable all cell phones and pagers in the audience. I hadn't realized it before, but one of the joys of speleology is that none of my caving partners can be reached a hundred feet under the ground.

chines. On the street, drivers and pedestrians dodge each other while talking over cell phones. In cafes, nerds type on laptops. Office managers bring their work home on floppy disks. The telecommuter merely represents one milestone in the blurring of home and office.

As work sneaks into playtime, play just isn't as much fun. Used to be that only students brought classwork home; increasingly, everyone has homework, everyone's on call. Our home provides little refuge from the stress of the outside world.

This isn't just the fault of technology—so many people want high-tech careers and professions that they willingly latch onto jobs which demand twenty-four-hour availability. And so we find the Webmaster who's on call all night, just in case the file server crashes. The high school teacher who answers students' e-mail all evening. The gardener who polishes her Web site when she comes home. For them, home is simply an extension of their workplace.

For children, home computers, instructional videotapes, and educational television extend the school into their home. Forget the innocence of childhood: Our kids are increasingly programmed as academic automatons.

The Internet is widely promoted as an aid for speed, profit, productivity, and efficiency. These business goals simply aren't the aims of a home. Maybe there's such a thing as kitchen productivity, but efficiency doesn't make much sense in my living room, and exactly who considers profits in their bedroom?

At home, our goals might include tranquillity, reflection,

and warmth . . . hardly the image brought up by the phrase "home computing." With houses increasingly wired for communications, electronic messages invade our home life. It's not just the telemarketers who disrupt dinner with sales and surveys. Rather, our private space is increasingly available to the outside world, whether it's a call from the boss, tonight's business news on the TV, or an e-mail message about a business meeting.

Nor are the goals of business those of a school. Productivity doesn't map onto a sixth-grade class in pre-algebra. It's absurd to speak of increasing the efficiency of an instructor teaching a third-grade student how salt melts ice. Will a 200 MHz computer educate a child twice as fast as a 100 MHz computer?

The way we communicate constrains how we interact. Computer networks provide chat rooms in which emotions must fit into eighty columns of ASCII text, punctuated by smiley faces. No longer need my correspondent begin a letter with a gratuitous "Dear Cliff." Rather, the header of the e-mail describes recipient, sender, and subject. Any pretense of politeness is erased by the cold efficiency of the medium.

One survey reports that office workers typically receive 190 messages per day. Yet computer network promoters tell us that we need ever faster links and constantly more connectivity. Will I get more work done today if I receive 300 messages rather than 200?

Instead of encouraging me to concentrate on a single job, the constant stream of electronic messages makes me constantly flip from one task to another. Computers are great at doing this, but people aren't. Promoters of electronic work-places may speak glowingly of living asynchronous lives, but most of my work requires concentration, thinking, and organization . . . hardly promoted by a river of electronic messages.

Getting a high-speed link to the Internet causes web pages to load faster. At first glance, you'd think that this would reduce the amount of time that students would spend on-line. Hardly. As connection speeds increase, college students spend more time surfing the Web, and less time writing, studying, or whatever they don't want to do. Same's true for office workers—an Internet link is a license to goof off.

As Robert Kraut and Vicki Lundmark's study reveals, e-mail enhances distant communications while degrading local interactions. It perniciously gives us the illusion of making friends with faraway strangers while taking our attention away from our friends, family, and neighbors.

In the past, people in trouble relied on close, nearby friends for support. Today, plenty of people turn to on-line support groups or chat rooms. Professor Mary Baker of Stanford reports that while she was expecting, she exchanged five e-mail messages a day with a friend across the country . . . a woman she'd never met. Yet e-mail pen pals can hardly provide the social support of a nearby friend or family member—if Professor Baker had to rush to the hospital, she could hardly get a ride from her e-mail friend.

Today, it's natural enough to look to the Internet for a community, since our real neighborhoods have been relentlessly undercut by television, automobiles, and urban renewal.

Yet as more and more people turn to the Internet, our real communities receive even less human investment.

For the effect of instant electronic communications is to isolate us from our colleagues next door. I met two computer jocks at a television station who spent their free time playing an Internet game with each other. Even though they sat five feet from each other, they'd communicate via e-mail and rarely so much as glanced at each other.

Professor Zimbardo tells me that sometimes he sticks his head into the office of a friend down the hall, with nothing more important than to say, "Hi!" "On several occasions, my greeting has been received with the shock of 'What's so important that you're invading my personal space? Why are you interrupting my productivity?'"

The price of computing at home—as in school and at work—is far more than the cost of the hardware. The opportunity cost is our time, and it is taken out of our individual lives and our very real neighborhoods. The time you spend behind the monitor could be spent facing another person across a table or across a tennis court. Disguised as efficiency machines, digital time bandits steal our lives and undermine our communities.

All Truth

t's an April evening in 1972. As Buffalo's steel mills gear up for the third shift, the University of Buffalo's campus bells chime out 9 P.M. From across campus floats the acrid sting of tear gas. It's a student riot, probably protesting the Vietnam war.

Not that I care. I'm heading home from the physics department, a stack of books under my arm. Statistical mechanics texts, chock full of details on thermodynamics and fluid flow. I'm cramming for next week's big exam.

As I walk across campus in the dusk, a policeman spots me. I give him a neutral smile and keep walking. He's equipped with the standard riot issue—helmet, leather jacket, tear gas rifle.

"Hey, student! Stop!" he shouts.

"Don't worry," I answer. "I'm just a physics jock. No rioter." I point to the stack of physics books under my arm. Cops chase looters, not scientist wannabes.

"You're a student," he reiterates, and aims his rifle at me. Whumph—he shoots a tear gas grenade at me. In slow motion, I watch this canister fly toward my face. It's the size of a Pepsi can, trailing a cloud of angry smoke. The can misses, but the gas hits home—half a breath and my throat clogs.

The cop's coming straight at me. My lungs sting—can't say anything. I wave my thermodynamics text at him. Makes no difference—he's after me with his rifle butt.

I drop the books and start running. Anywhere. Past chestnut trees and parking meters. Across a weedy lawn. The cop's right behind me. Tear gas might stop your lungs, but not your feet.

The cop's chasing, but all that cop gear slows him down. I dodge into an open window and lose the guy. One glance and I realize I'm in Hayes Hall, the administration building, capped by a venerable old clock tower.

The hallway's lit only by exit signs, so while the cop fumbles at the window, I run up a staircase. A minute later, I'm up three floors.

My heart's pounding and my lungs burn. What am I doing here? I just want to study physics.

In the shadows of the hallway, I see a little access door, maybe a meter high. The kind that might lead to a ventilator shaft. I twiddle the latch; it pops open. Inside, it smells like a century of dust. It's dark—no exit signs—but a soft glow trickles down from above. A wooden staircase without railings leads up.

I've stumbled onto the door to the bell tower! I shinny through the hole and latch the door behind me. Gingerly, I climb the stairs, my mind flashing images of Alfred Hitchcock's *Vertigo*. Let the cops try to find me here.

Two flights up, I hear a steady tic, tic, tic. Lead weights drive a handful of brass gears and a ratchety escapement wheel. A pendulum, maybe three feet long, keeps the mechanism running, ticking off the seconds. It's the clockwork that drives the big clocks on the outside.

Hey—I remember that from physics—a one-meter pendulum ticks once a second. And its frequency varies inversely with the square root of the pendulum's length. That's why I'm here: to learn physics.

A six-foot-long wooden dowel extends from the top of the clock. I climb the stairs to a platform where a differential gear splits into four rods, each going to a different clock face. North, east, west, and south . . . the four clocks look out over the campus. From behind, I can read the time backward. It's almost ten at night. What am I doing here?

A wooden ladder extends up from the platform . . . it's not at all stable, but I'm game. I climb ten rungs, push open a hatchway, and squeeze out.

I'm inside the cupola at the top of the bell tower. Next to me, four bells, each about four feet high . . . these are the hourly chimes! A breeze blows through chicken wire and I can look down and across campus. Over by Main Street, a mob of students is heaving bricks at the police. Tear gas grenades spout smoke. Cops ducking behind cars with blinking lights. Screams and curses.

It's ten at night. I should be studying physics. What am I doing here?

I hear the clockwork below me creak into action. By my feet, four hammers cock back, ready to strike the bells. Loudly, the bells ring out the Westminster sequence. Then the biggest bell slowly tolls ten times. What am I doing here?

In the reflected moonlight, I can discern an engraving on one of the bells. With my coat, I wipe off the dirt, and slowly make out an inscription, unseen for the past fifty years. Yes. That's why I'm here:

> *All truth is one.*
> *In this light, may science and religion endeavor*
> *   for the steady evolution of Mankind:*
> *From darkness to light,*
> *From prejudice to tolerance,*
> *From narrowness to broadmindedness.*
> *It is the voice of life which calls you.*
> *Come and learn.*

Index with an Attitude

Index with an Attitude